done in a day...
Fantastic Fix-ups

done in a day
Fantastic Fix-ups

STEWART WALTON

TIME®
LIFE
BOOKS

Alexandria, Virginia

TIME LIFE BOOKS

Time-Life Books is a division of Time Life Inc.

TIME LIFE INC
President and CEO: George Artandi
TIME-LIFE BOOKS
President: Stephen R. Frary
TIME-LIFE CUSTOM PUBLISHING
Vice President and Publisher: Terry Newell
Vice President of Sales and Marketing: Neil Levin
Director of Special Sales: Liz Ziehl
Project Manager: Jennie Halfant
Director of Acquisitions: Jennifer Pearce
Director of Design: Christopher M. Register

Time-Life is a trademark of Time Warner Inc. U.S.A.

Library of Congress Cataloging-in-Publication Data
Walton, Stewart.
    Fantastic fix-ups / by Stewart Walton.
        p. cm. -- (Done in a Day)
    Includes index
    ISBN 0-7835-5309-9 (alk. paper)
    1. Handicraft. 2. House furnishings. 3. Interior decoration.
I. Title. II. Series.
TT157.W3557   1998
745.5--DC21   98-18455
                            CIP

A Marshall Edition. Conceived, edited and designed by Marshall Editions Ltd
The Orangery, 161 New Bond Street
London W1Y 9PA

First published in the UK in 1998 by Marshall Publishing Ltd
Copyright © 1998 Marshall Editions Developments Ltd
All right reserved including the right of reproduction in whole or in part
in any form

Project Editor: Esther Labi
Designer: Bridgewater Books
Consultant: Sally Walton
Art Director: Sean Keogh
DTP Editor: Lesley Gilbert
Managing Editor: Clare Currie
Editorial Coordinator: Rebecca Clunes
Production: James Bann
Photographer Graham Rae

Originated in Singapore by Master Image   Printed and bound in Italy

CONTENTS

INTRODUCTION

Remember that awful old lamp base that has been hidden away on the top shelf for years, the useful cupboard your kind, but misguided Aunt donated to your first apartment, or that old table spoiled by coffee stains? Don't throw them away until you've read this book...

The following pages will show you how to breathe new life into furniture and accessories that have long passed their prime, in only one day. Inspiration and instruction are given in the form of step-by-step photography and simple structured text, ensuring that everything goes according to plan.

You can start by looking through the book for an idea that you like, or find the object first and it's potential will become apparent as you read through the book. Finding something to fix up isn't as difficult as you think. Take a look around your home – you will probably find a few objects that need brightening up. Otherwise, scouring junk stores for that one piece with lots of potential is a creative task in itself!

Guiding you carefully from start to finish, each project begins with a list of materials and equipment you need, as well as suggestions on how to work out how much you need to buy and where to buy any unusual items. All the tools and equipment you need can be easily obtained from DIY stores, or hobby and craft stores. When buying necessary materials and equipment, try a general DIY store first – if they stock what you are searching for, it is likely to cost less than at a specialty store. Also, many DIY stores now stock a range of craft materials associated with home improvement. Many craft products are also available by mail order; and if you need addresses, look at the advertisements in the back of craft or home-improvement magazines for potential suppliers.

However, if it's practical advice you're looking for, go to a specialty store, where you will have more chance of finding staff with both the time and knowledge to help you. If you still don't feel confident enough to start, do some further reading on a particular technique and if you have time, indulge in some practice beforehand. For example, try some of the painting techniques featured in this book, such as stamping or stenciling, on a piece of thick card or plywood first. That way, you can see how the colors you have chosen look together and how the effect will look in your home.

If you love working with paint, there are stencils and templates provided for you to use in stenciling projects, as well as a simple stamp made out of household sponge, but you can always design your own stencils and stamps to suit the rest of your decor. As you progress, try more detailed patterns that incorporate several colors. There are also freehand painting projects for you to try if you don't care for the restrictions of a stencil or stamp. If painting is not your forte, there's simple spray-painting, gilding, decoupage, and even an easy mosaic to try.

This book can be either loosely followed, or followed to the letter. If you like one particular aspect of a project, use it as a starting point to develop your own ideas, or try it out on an entirely separate accessory or surface. Try to select an object that has something in common with the one we have used in the project, either the material, the shape, or the function. Experiment with your favorite colors until you find the combination that perfectly complements the surrounding environment. You can also try using the techniques in this book on larger and more adventurous objects as you become more confident and skillful.

Fantastic Fix-ups has twelve exciting projects to try, so you are sure to find something you like. Brighten up old **storage tins** and learn basic free-hand painting techniques. Or try stenciling, including **stenciled borders** and a **stenciled chair**, where you make your own stencil. For larger pieces of furniture, there's the simple **combed side table** or the **wood-grain effect chest**. If you're looking for something a little brighter, why not try colorful **planters** or the **painted lamp bases**? For an aged antique effect, the **print room firescreen** or the **gilded picture frames** are perfect, and if you're looking for a fun storage solution, the **toy chest** may be the answer for you. For a more hands-on approach, try the **mosaic table top**, or make a new **scalloped lampshade** for an old lamp base.

Whatever you choose to do, this book is packed with clever ideas so that soon you'll be able to create family heirlooms from items that were once earmarked for the scrap heap.

Now that you are ready to attempt your first project, keep the following safety procedures in mind at all times:

❖ Several of the projects suggest protective clothing for certain steps so please wear them. Remember, accidents do happen;

❖ Always keep powertools unplugged while they are not in use;

❖ If you are working outdoors, make sure that any powertool cables are kept clear of water;

❖ When working with a craft knife, keep your steadying hand *behind* and *well away* from your cutting hand;

❖ Wear goggles when breaking ceramic tiles for the mosaic table top (project 10);

❖ Only cut MDF (Medium Density Fiberboard) in a well-ventilated area and wear the correct type of breathing mask.

HOW THE BOOK WORKS

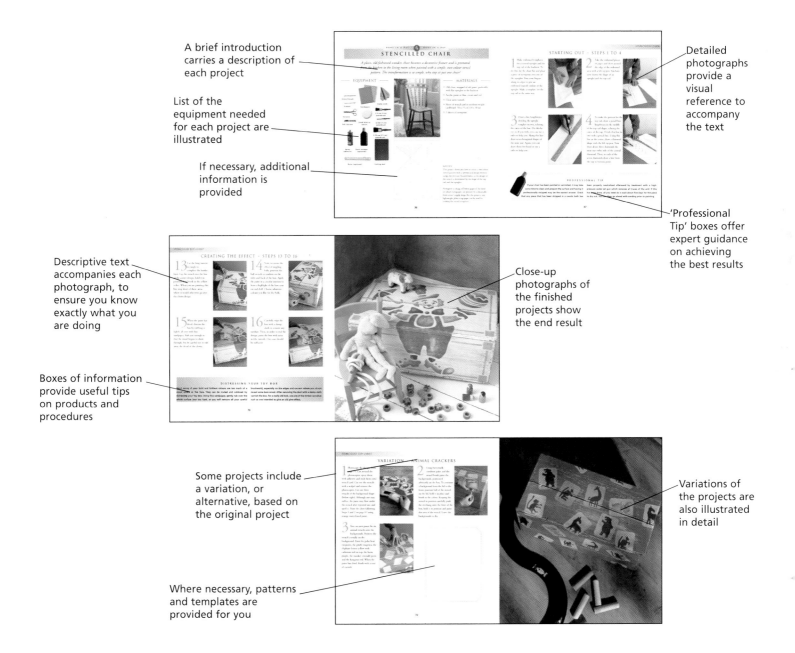

A brief introduction carries a description of each project

List of the equipment needed for each project are illustrated

If necessary, additional information is provided

Descriptive text accompanies each photograph, to ensure you know exactly what you are doing

Boxes of information provide useful tips on products and procedures

Some projects include a variation, or alternative, based on the original project

Where necessary, patterns and templates are provided for you

Detailed photographs provide a visual reference to accompany the text

'Professional Tip' boxes offer expert guidance on achieving the best results

Close-up photographs of the finished projects show the end result

Variations of the projects are also illustrated in detail

PAINTED STORAGE TINS

This painting project is in keeping with the folk art tradition of decorating household utensils, and can be used to decorate old or new tins. Once you have mastered the technique of transfer painting, try painting other objects in your home, such as picture or mirror frames.

EQUIPMENT

Sable paintbrushes Nos. 1, 5, and 8

1-inch paintbrush

Pencil

Scissors

2 small dishes or saucers for mixing paint

Low-tack masking tape

Fine-gauge steel wool

Rubbing alcohol

MATERIALS

❖ 2 storage tins, the ones used here measure 8-inches high and 5¾-inches high

❖ Acrylic paint in Indian red, vermilion, burnt sienna, cadmium red, white, black, lemon yellow, burnt umber, and green

❖ P.v.a. (white) glue

❖ Shellac

❖ Transfer paper (with chalk backing)

❖ Strip of paper, at least as long as circumference of larger tin

❖ Sheet of 8½ x 11-inch paper

NOTES

If you don't have low-tack masking tape, you can reduce the tackiness of a piece of ordinary masking tape by sticking it onto an item of clothing and then quickly pulling it off again. When you use the piece of masking tape, it will be easy to remove and will not leave any sticky residue.

Transfer paper is available from craft stores and is sold in sheets or rolls. Make sure that you choose a chalky transfer paper, not a waxy carbon one which would repel paint.

Methylated spirits (rubbing alcohol) is available from craft or hardware stores and is an excellent cleaner for brushes used with varnish.

STARTING OUT – STEPS 1 TO 4

1 Roughen the surface of the larger storage tin with the steel wool. In a dish, mix equal parts of Indian red and burnt sienna paint, then add just a touch of cadmium red. Add enough water so that the paint runs off the brush and, using a 1-inch paintbrush, paint the tin and lid in one direction to avoid brush marks. Allow to dry, then rub the tin and lid with steel wool and give them another coat of paint. Allow them to dry.

2 Trace the pattern on page 15 onto a piece of paper, or choose your own design (see below). Make sure the design is big enough to fill the space between the rim and the bottom of the tin. Place a piece of transfer paper underneath your traced pattern and stick both sheets onto the tin, holding them in place with low-tack masking tape.

3 Slowly draw over your traced design with a pencil. When you have finished, carefully take off both pieces of paper to reveal the design in chalk on the side of the tin.

4 In a saucer, mix together 5 parts white and 1 part burnt umber acrylic paint. Add enough water to the mixture so that the paint runs off the brush easily.

CHOOSING YOUR OWN DESIGN

As well as tracing the designs on page 15, you can use any of the other designs in this book or copy a design from wallpaper, fabric, or from a magazine. In order to get the design to the required size for transferring, enlarge or reduce the original on a photocopier.

Unlike stenciling, where simplicity is the keynote, the design you choose can be relatively complicated, with fine lines or intricate detail. Your brushstrokes will provide the flourishes, so just trace the basic pattern shapes.

CREATING THE EFFECT – STEPS 5 TO 8

5 Get yourself into a comfortable position so that you can keep your hand steady. Then, using a No. 5 sable paintbrush, paint the "petals" of the design in one continuous stroke, taking care not to paint over the outline onto the background (see "Painting Technique" below).

6 Using the smallest sable paintbrush (No. 1), paint the stem of the flower with one stroke of the brush. Leave the white paint to dry and wash the brush and saucer.

7 In a clean saucer, mix some black paint with enough water so that the paint runs smoothly off the brush. Paint one side of each petal, the center of the flower and the leaves on one side of the stem. Set the black paint aside.

8 In another saucer, mix up some lemon-yellow paint and some water as before. Use the No. 8 sable brush to paint the leaves on the stem with the same painting technique. Then use the No. 1 brush to paint a yellow line in between the petals. With one stroke, start at the center of the flower and follow the edge of the petal. Leave the tin to dry and wash the saucer and brushes.

PAINTING TECHNIQUE

Successful transfer painting relies on the application of paint in one continuous brushstroke. You need good-quality, clean sable brushes, a steady hand, and carefully diluted paint. By applying the paint in one continuous motion you do not leave brushstrokes and are left with a smooth finish. Keep practicing the brushstrokes until the paint flows perfectly from the brush. Don't rush. For a more translucent finish, mix equal parts of paint and p.v.a. glue. Dilute with water as necessary.

CREATING THE EFFECT - STEPS 9 TO 12

9 While the tin is drying, paint the lid. Using the No. 1 sable brush, paint a black line around the top and the rim of the lid. As you paint, keep each line an even thickness all the way around. Take care to keep each line the same distance from the top and rim to ensure the ends of the line meet up.

10 To decorate the lid, cut a strip of paper to the height of the lid. Wrap the strip of paper around the lid and make a pencil mark where the two ends meet.

11 Cut the paper along this mark so that the strip of paper is now the exact length of the circumference. Fold the strip in half, then fold in half again and finally once again, so that the piece of paper has now been divided into eighths.

12 Wrap the strip of paper around the lid so that the edge of the strip of paper is centered between the two black lines painted on the rim. Make a light pencil mark on the lid at each fold, so that the lid is divided into eight sections.

CARING FOR YOUR BRUSHES

Good-quality sable paintbrushes of varying sizes are probably indispensable if you want to produce a truly professional finish in any finely detailed painting you choose to do. They are, however, extremely expensive and for most purposes synthetic hair brushes make an acceptable substitute. All brushes last longer if you care for them properly, and this obviously makes sense if you have invested in sable. Wash them immediately after use and store them in jars, standing upright so that the tip is not pressed out of shape.

CREATING THE EFFECT - STAGES 13 TO 16

13 Mix up more lemon-yellow paint and water if necessary; then using the No. 1 sable brush, paint a short line between two pencil marks. Make the line thin at one end and thick at the other, painting in one continuous stroke. Continue painting alternate sections around the lid in the same way.

14 To complete the design, paint two diagonal lines, starting from just beyond the end of one line to the midway point of the next. Paint these lines in the same way, thin at one end and thick at the other, in one continuous brushstroke. Continue painting until the lid is completed, taking care not to smudge the wet paint. Allow the paint to dry.

15 When the paint on the storage tin is dry, lightly rub the surface with steel wool. Make sure you do not rub too hard and vigorously or you will rub away the design.

16 To achieve an antiqued effect, paint a coat of shellac on the lid and the tin with the 1-inch paintbrush. Clean the brush with rubbing alcohol.

CRACKLE GLAZE

Your storage tins can also be treated with crackle glaze to give them an interesting and convincing aged effect. Special crackle varnish is applied in two coats, which, because of their different drying speeds, interact to produce fine cracks when the second varnish dries. Using a hair dryer to speed the drying process will emphasize the cracks. When the crackled coat is dry, gently rub color into the cracks using a little oil-based paint; raw umber is a color often chosen for this purpose.

FINISHING IT OFF - STEPS 17 TO 20

17 Rub over the surface of the small tin with steel wool. Using the 1-inch paintbrush, paint the storage tin with two coats of burnt umber, allowing each coat to dry. Transfer the design on page 15 onto the side of the tin as shown in Steps 2–3. In a saucer, dilute some vermilion red paint with water as in Step 4. For a translucent paint effect, mix together equal amounts of p.v.a. glue and paint before diluting.

18 Using a No. 5 sable brush, paint a dot in the center of the lid and then paint some "petals" radiating from it. Start near the edge of the lid and pull the brush back to the middle in one movement. Leave enough room between each red petal to paint a green one. On the tin, paint the center of the design and a pair of diagonally opposite "leaves" with the red paint. Remember, apply the paint in one stroke.

19 Wash the brush in water. Using a clean saucer, mix some p.v.a. glue with green paint as in Step 17. On the lid, paint green petals in between the red ones and paint a straight and even strip around the side of the lid. On the tin, paint the other diagonal set of "leaves" of the design with the No. 5 sable brush. Clean the saucer and brush and leave the storage tin to dry.

20 Mix together some white paint and p.v.a. glue in a saucer, as before. With the No. 1 brush, add highlights to the petals on the tin and the lid, and add a highlight to the central circle of the lid. When the paint is dry lightly rub over the surface of the tin and lid with steel wool and then paint them both with a coat of shellac. Clean the brush with rubbing alcohol and allow the storage tin to dry.

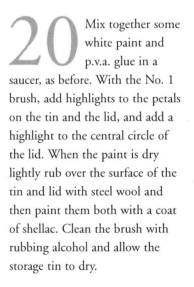

COLOR VARIATIONS

You do not have to follow the exact color combination used here. Experiment with different shades of color and different color combinations by painting onto paper or cardboard first. You can create a large number of different shades simply by adding a little bit of another color to your main color. When you are happy with the colors you have chosen, you can paint your storage tins. However, if you change your mind about the colors you have chosen, acrylic paint dries quickly and can easily be painted over.

STENCILED BORDERS

Coordinate your interiors by stenciling border designs on to different surfaces. Here chairs, walls, curtains, and even a picture frame are linked by a discreet geometric design. It looks intricate but is easy to make, thanks to all those straight lines.

EQUIPMENT

Iron

Stencil brush

Craft knife

Pencil

Hairdryer

Spool of cotton thread

Damp cloth

Metal ruler

Sandpaper

1¼-inch paintbrush

Spray adhesive

Small dish or saucer for mixing paint

Tape measure

Adhesive tape or masking tape

Scissors

Cutting mat

MATERIALS

❖ Length of curtain, the one used here measures 43 x 53 inches

❖ Picture frame, the one used here measures 10¾ x 12¾ inches

❖ Stencil card, 19¾ x 30 inches

❖ Water-base paint in off-white

❖ Acrylic paint in opaque oxide of chromium (green), raw sienna, white, and ultramarine

❖ Matte or satin acrylic varnish

❖ P.v.a. (white) glue

❖ Sheet of 8½ x 14-inch paper

NOTES

All the designs used are on pages 26 and 27. The patterns are based on a mosaic theme but, if they do not appeal to you, you can make your own. One alternative would be to use a photocopy of a piece of lacework and enlarge it for use as a basis for your stencil design.

Apply a light coating of spray adhesive to the back of the stencil before you start. This one coat will be sufficient to complete the project. Glue is not suitable, as you have to be able to remove them.

STARTING OUT – STEPS 1 TO 4

1 To make the wall stencil, you need to photocopy the design on page 27, enlarging or reducing it to the size you want. Then make four photocopies of the design, one for each of the colors you will be using. (If you trim down the photocopies, make sure you do not cut them along the two straight lines at the edge of the design.) Spray the back of each copy with spray adhesive.

2 Cut out four pieces of stencil card, making them slightly larger than the photocopies. Stick down each copy of the design onto a piece of stencil card.

3 It is important that all the stencils are the same width, as this will ensure that they are aligned when you stencil the wall. To make sure each stencil is equal in width, use a metal ruler and craft knife to cut along the two straight lines on the top and bottom of each stencil. Protect your work surface by using a cutting mat.

4 The four designs are now ready to be cut out with the craft knife, but take care to keep your non-cutting hand at a safe distance from the blade. First cut out the registration marks (see below) and then cut out only the triangular shapes of one of the stencils.

REGISTRATION MARKS

Registration marks are a segment of the continuing stencil pattern and allow you to place different stencils in the same position. You need them, for example, when you are using more than one color. They also allow you to position the stencil accurately next to the area you have just stenciled, allowing you to continue your stencil pattern neatly, without any unsightly gaps. If you are using your own stencil design, choose a suitable part of the design to act as registration marks and don't forget to cut the marks on each stencil.

CREATING THE EFFECT – STEPS 5 TO 8

5 Using another piece of stencil card, cut out only the wavy borders of the design. (There is no need to cut out registration marks on this stencil because it will easily align with the painted border design on the wall.)

6 On a third stencil card, cut out each of the four inner circles. Finally, on the last stencil card, cut out the four outer circles. Don't forget to cut out the registration marks on these two stencils.

7 Make sure all your stencils are facing the right way (with the registration marks on the left) and then make a diagonal cut across the top right-hand corner of each stencil. This will indicate the top of each of the stencils.

8 You can now peel off the photocopied design from each of the stencils. Without the photocopied designs, it is impossible to tell which side of the stencils is the right side up. This is why it is important to mark the top of each stencil.

COLOR COORDINATES

The colors used in this stencil design will be determined by the decor of your existing room, and also by the color of the curtains. Complementary colors, such as red/green, blue/orange, and yellow/purple, give the strongest contrasts. These can be softened by the addition of white to make pastel colors. Try out your color scheme on some scrap paper first, before you commit it to your walls. However many colors you choose, remember, you must have one stencil for each color.

CREATING THE EFFECT ~ STEPS 9 TO 12

9 Using a tape measure, measure the height of the border from the floor; 36 inches is usually a good height. With a pencil, lightly make a mark at each end of the wall at your chosen height. If you are stenciling a long wall or a whole room, you may want to make several marks along the wall.

10 To make a guideline, so that the stencil will be in a straight line, fix one end of a thread on a pencil mark with a piece of adhesive tape. Then, unwind the spool to the other mark at the end of the wall and tape it in place. It is important to keep the thread taut, so it may be necessary to tape it in several places on the wall.

11 Lightly coat the back of the wavy-border stencil with spray adhesive. The stencil only needs to be slightly tacky so do not spray on too much. Position the bottom of the stencil on top of the length of thread and press the stencil onto the wall (see below).

12 In a small dish or saucer, mix some ultramarine and white acrylic paint to get a very pale blue. You will need to make enough to stencil the border design as well as the large circles. Using the stencil brush loaded with very little paint, use a dabbing or circular motion to paint the wavy stencil borders onto the wall.

PROFESSIONAL TIP

If you are stenciling a whole room, choose your starting point carefully. If you are an absolute beginner, it is probably sensible to start off behind a door or a large piece of furniture, where any mistakes you make while you get the hang of things will not be too obvious. Nothing looks worse than a stencil that goes off course in such a way that the start and finish do not match up precisely. You can avoid glaring problems by starting and finishing at a wall corner, in a doorway or at a window frame.

FINISHING IT OFF — STEPS 13 TO 16

13 Carefully lift the stencil off and reposition it so that the end of the wavy line overlaps onto the painted wavy line. Make sure the stencil is resting on the thread, and then continue painting. When you reach a corner, bend the stencil at a right angle so it rests on the thread on the other wall. Continue until you have painted the border on all the walls and set the paint aside (see below).

14 Wash the stencil brush. Apply a light coat of spray adhesive to the back of the stencil with the triangles cut out. Position it at the start of the frieze on top of the thread and press it on the wall. In a small dish, mix some green and white acrylic paint. Paint in the triangles with the stencil brush as before. Use the registration marks to reposition the stencil and continue stenciling the design around the room.

15 Wash the brush and set the green paint aside for the next step. Position the stencil with the large circles cut out at the start of the frieze, making sure that the registration marks fit over the triangular design. Using the stencil brush and the pale blue paint, stencil the large circles until you have completed all the walls.

16 Rest the stencil with the smaller circles cut out on the thread at the start of the frieze. Position the registration marks over those of the triangular design as before. Using the stencil brush and the green paint, stencil the small circles and continue around the room. Wash the stencil brush in water when you have finished.

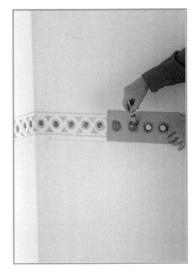

STENCIL PAINT

Acrylic paints are always used in stenciling because they dry so quickly. By the time you finish the room, the first painted design will be dry, but always check first. If the paint is not dry, it may stick to the next stencil you place on top of it. You can use a hairdryer to dry the paint more quickly. You can also buy special stencil paint, which is usually sold in sticks. This paint is oil-based to prevent the stick from drying out. However, it dries quickly when it is used, since you need to use only a very small quantity at a time.

STENCILED FRAME – STEPS 1 TO 4

1 Roughen the surface of the picture frame with sandpaper and wipe off the dust with a damp cloth. In a small dish or saucer, mix some off-white paint with an equal amount of water. Paint the frame with one coat of the thinned paint and leave to dry. Meanwhile, on a photocopier, reduce or enlarge the top design on page 27 so that it fits your frame. Then prepare the stencil and cut out the pattern as before.

2 This pattern works best if you stencil the corners first. Spray the back of the stencil with a light coating of spray adhesive, then position the square part of the design over one corner and press it down. Use the stencil brush to paint the design with green paint (opaque oxide of chromium) straight from the tube. Lift the stencil off and repeat on each corner. Allow to dry for five minutes or so.

3 To stencil each side, position the longer part of the design so that it butts up against the corner design. Press it down in position and paint the stencil. Lift off and reposition the stencil by aligning it with what you have just painted. When you come to the end of one side, place a piece of paper over the painted corner so that you do not stencil over it.

4 Once the corner design is masked out, position the stencil and paint over it. Continue painting the rest of the frame the same way, masking out each corner. When you have finished stenciling the frame, make sure the paint is dry before giving it a coat of acrylic varnish.

STENCILING FABRICS

You can use the technique of stenciling on many different surfaces, such as paper, wood, or walls. If you stencil fabric, it can then be made into curtains or into other items of soft furnishing, including cushion covers or an armchair cover. Try stenciling a border of ivy leaves on a simple white tablecloth or a border of roses on a valance. When stenciling fabric, special fabric paint can also be used, if you intend to machine wash the item. If the fabric is dryclean only, use p.v.a. glue mixed with the paint to stencil the fabric.

STENCILED CURTAINS – STEPS 1 TO 4

1 Before stenciling, make sure the fabric is absolutely flat. Prepare the curtain (or other fabric) by ironing it to get rid of any creases. Lay the curtain on a flat work surface and let it cool down. Meanwhile, prepare the stencil as before, following the technique described in Steps 1 to 8 on pages 19-20, but this time using the design on page 26.

2 In a small dish, mix up three parts green paint, one part ultramarine paint, and one part p.v.a. glue. Spray adhesive lightly on the back of the stencil, and position it near the bottom of the curtain, overlapping the edge slightly. This gives the impression that the design goes around the back of the curtain. Check that the stencil is straight (see below) and keep the material taut as you stencil it.

3 Remove the stencil and place it next to the painted design so that the first top and bottom cutout squares are over the top and bottom painted squares on the curtain. Slowly lay the stencil down.

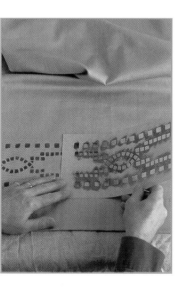

4 Next, make sure that the stencil is straight using a ruler or a scrap of card. Continue stenciling the rest of curtain until the border design is complete.

PROFESSIONAL TIP

When stenciling borders, it is particularly important that the pattern remain completely straight. When stenciling the curtain, use a ruler to make sure that both ends of the stencil are at an equal distance from the bottom of the curtain. An even easier method is to use a piece of cardboard or stencil card cut to the same measurement as the distance between the curtain edge and the stencil. Keep the card aligned with the fabric edge and slide the stencil along it.

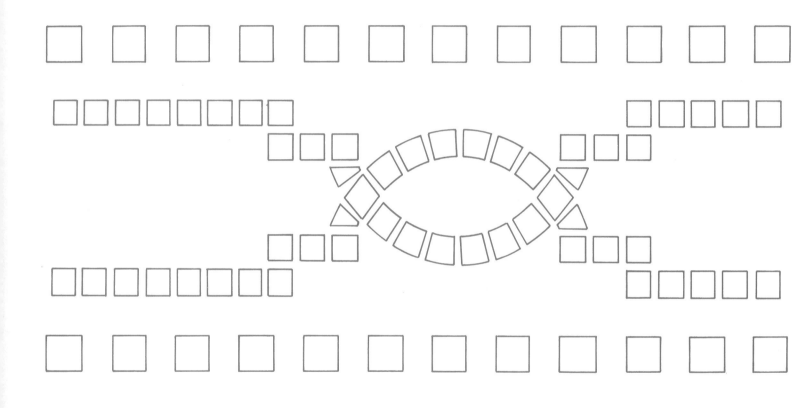

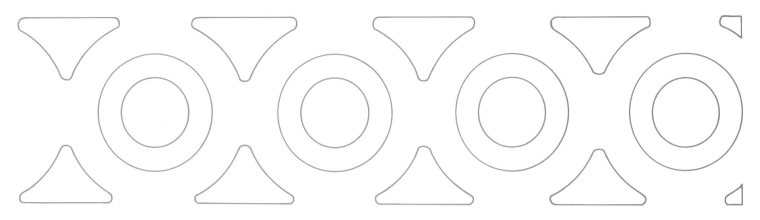

INDOOR PLANTERS AND TROUGHS

Plain terra-cotta pots or planters take a new lease on life with simple painted decorations. A cheap and highly individual alternative to expensive "jardinières", they provide an opportunity to use up any water-base paint left over from home decorating.

EQUIPMENT

2 small dishes for mixing paint

Scissors

Pencil

Craft knife

Ruler

1-inch paintbrush

Rubber band

Tape measure

No. 8 sable paintbrush or synthetic hair paintbrush

Plate large enough to stand plant pot on

Newspaper

Spray adhesive

Thick household sponge

Paper

MATERIALS

❖ 3 terra-cotta plant pots

❖ Acrylic paint in cream, green, yellow, and white

❖ P.v.a. (white) glue

❖ Square sheet of paper, larger than diameter of pot

VARIATION

❖ Metal, plastic, or wooden plant trough (The one used for this project is metal)

❖ Primer (if using a metal trough)

❖ Matte black spray paint

❖ Acrylic paint in white

NOTE

This is a good way to use up the dregs of emulsion paint that are usually left over after decorating the house, or alternatively, you can also buy small test pots of emulsion.

STARTING OUT - STEPS 1 TO 4

1 Take a square sheet of paper and turn the pot upside down on it. Using a ruler to help you, position the pot equidistant from each side of the paper. Draw a line all the way around the circumference of the pot, resting your pencil against the rim of the pot. Turn the pot right side up and position it in the center of the circle you have just drawn, using a ruler to check this. Draw another circle on the paper around the bottom of the pot.

2 With a ruler and a pencil, divide the square of paper into quarters, drawing the lines so they overlap the outside circle. Next, draw two diagonal lines from corner to corner creating eight segments. Finally, divide each of these eighths in two, to create 16 segments.

3 With the scissors, cut around the outer circle, and then cut around the inner circle, about 1 inch away from the pencil line that you have drawn.

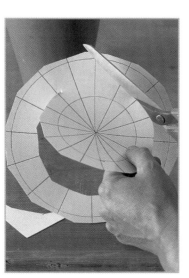

4 In a saucer, combine the cream-colored paint with a little p.v.a. glue, mix to a smooth consistency, and paint the outside of the pot, taking care not to paint the rim. Allow the pot to dry thoroughly.

PAINTING WITH P.V.A. GLUE

Adding p.v.a. glue to acrylic paint will seal the surface of the terra-cotta pots, preventing the paint from soaking into the terra-cotta, which is porous. (The greater the percentage of p.v.a. glue, the more transparent the final paint color will be.) However, the final finish is not sealed and the pots will acquire an aged patina if you put them outside. If you wish to preserve the vibrancy of the color on the pots, and intend to keep them outside, weatherproof them with a coat of clear polyurethane varnish after the paint has dried.

CREATING THE EFFECT - STEPS 5 TO 8

5 Place the pot on the smaller cutout circle and place the larger circle on the top so that the lines on this circle align with those on the circle below. When they are aligned, lightly mark the positions of these lines around the top and bottom of the plant pot with a pencil. Make sure that you do not inadvertently move either sheet of paper.

6 Take the tape measure or ruler and place it on the side of the pot so that each end of the tape measure is lined up with the marks at top and bottom. Holding the pot still, make a light pencil mark on the surface every inch along the length of the tape measure. Repeat this procedure on the opposite side of the pot.

7 Mix two parts of p.v.a. glue with one part of green paint in a saucer and add a little water until you reach an easy, flowing consistency.

8 To paint straight lines around the pot, place a rubber band around the pot slightly below the top pencil marks that you made in Step 6. Make sure the rubber band is laid out flat and that it is the same distance all the way around from the top.

PROFESSIONAL TIP

The joy of hand-painting will be spoiled if you get too hung up on producing perfectly straight lines. Indeed you are more likely to wobble if you worry. By all means, follow the rubber band technique outlined above, but just go with the flow; if your lines are not perfect, it doesn't matter. An alternative to the rubber band (if you want one) would be to position your pot on a lazy Susan (spinning circular surface usually found on dinner tables) or, if you have one, an old phonograph turntable, and spin it while you hold the brush.

CREATING THE EFFECT – STEPS 9 TO 12

9 Use the No. 8 sable brush to paint lines around the pot. Start on the top pencil mark and go around the pot, slowly turning it around in your hand while keeping the line you are painting the same distance from the rubber band. Press the brush slightly so that it splays out to create an even width of line. Reposition the rubber band as necessary to paint the rest of the lines around the pot.

10 To paint the vertical lines, start at the top and place the brush on one of the pencil marks around the rim. Pull the brush down in one movement so that the painted line joins up with the corresponding pencil mark on the bottom. When all the vertical lines are painted, the pot is finished and should be left to dry. Remember to wash your brush and saucer.

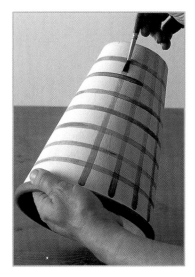

11 To paint the second pot, mix some p.v.a. glue with yellow paint in a saucer, but do not dilute it with water. Brush a thick coat of paint onto the pot, omitting the rim. Allow the pot to dry thoroughly.

12 When the base coat is completely dry, combine two parts of p.v.a. glue with one part of green paint in a saucer, add some water, and mix until the paint has a thin consistency. Load the clean No. 8 sable brush with paint and, holding the pot on its side, brush on a generous line around the underside of the rim.

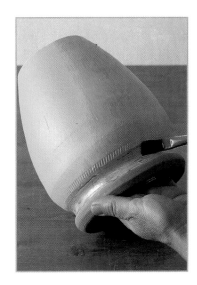

COLOR-COORDINATE YOUR PLANTS AND POTS

If you have a particular plant in mind for your pot, select colors that will contrast with or complement the color of your plant. For a vibrant red chili plant, for example, try painting your pot white checked with bright blue paint. Or, for a pot full of stargazer lilies, try painting your pot a soft creamy yellow with thinned lilac paint running down the sides. Or paint a pot bright orange and stamp it with yellow and white diamond shapes to brighten up an evergreen such as *Spathyphyllum* (peace lily) when it isn't flowering.

FINISHING IT OFF – STEPS 13 TO 16

13 Stand the pot on a plate and overload the brush with green paint. Then push the brush under the rim, on the line just painted. Hold the brush in position and let the paint run down the side of the pot. Repeat around the top of the pot. Overload the brush each time, to achieve the dripping paint effect. Leave the pot to dry.

14 To make a stamp for the third pot, cut out a 1-inch square from a thick household sponge. For a straight edge, it is best to use a craft knife. Decide how your diamond pattern will fit evenly around the rim. Depending on the size of your pot, your diamond shapes will butt up next to each other, or will be slightly separated.

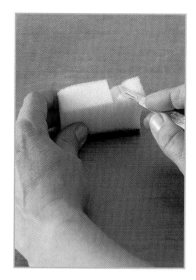

15 Mix up some green paint and p.v.a. glue in a saucer. Do not add any water as the paint must be thick. Omitting the rim, brush on the paint until the brush becomes dry, leaving areas that are barely covered with paint. Do not reload the brush as there is no need to cover the entire surface of the pot. Next, mix up some cream paint with p.v.a. glue and a little water in a saucer. Dip the sponge in so that it soaks up the paint.

16 Hold the pot upside down with the rim toward you. Position the loaded sponge so that the corners are in the middle of the rim to form a diamond shape. Push the sponge gently but firmly onto the pot. Reload the sponge with paint and continue around the top (see below).

PROFESSIONAL TIP

When using a sponge to stamp on a pattern, the paint should be the consistency of heavy cream. If it is too thin, the paint will run when you remove the sponge, ruining your pattern. If the paint is too thick, it will be too thick on the pot.

Don't press too hard with the sponge as this will release too much paint. Try out your stamp on a scrap piece of cardboard first, and experiment with different sponge pressures and paint thicknesses. You can then dilute or thicken your paint accordingly.

VARIATION – FUNKY GIRAFFE TROUGH

1 Clean the plant trough and, if it is metal (as this one is), paint it inside and out with rust-proof primer. When the primer has dried, paint the trough with the white water-base acrylic paint. Tear the paper into strips about 2 inches wide. Then tear the strips into squares, roughly 2- by 2-inches.

2 Choose a well-ventilated place to work in. Place the squares of paper on sheets of newspaper. Give them a coat of spray adhesive (see below). Stick the pieces of paper onto the trough, pressing the pieces down flat and leaving gaps between them. Fold the edges of the paper over the edge of the trough, and stick them down on the underside.

3 Before you spray-paint the trough, make sure that you are working in a well-ventilated area and protect the surrounding area with newspaper. Spray the sides of the trough with matte black spray paint. When using the spray paint, spray in short bursts and coat the sides evenly—this will avoid creating drips (see below).

4 When the paint has dried, carefully peel away each piece of paper, prying up an edge of each piece with the blade of a craft knife. It is important that you do not leave the pieces on too long as they will be stuck firm and difficult to remove. If you have a stand for your trough, you could spray the stand with gold paint as a finishing touch. Make sure you do this in a well-ventilated area.

PROFESSIONAL TIP

Spray adhesive and spray paint are useful when you need an even coating, but remember to always work in a well-ventilated area and protect your surroundings with plenty of newspaper. If you are using spray adhesive on paper that you have to remove and stick down again, use only a light coating applied in short bursts. However, take care that you do not blow your paper away. Similarly, when working with spray paint, use short bursts for an even coat. If the spray lingers on one spot, droplets will form on the surface.

STENCILED CHAIR

A plain, old-fashioned wooden chair becomes a decorative feature and is promoted from the kitchen to the living room when painted with a simple, two-color stencil pattern. Once you've transformed a single chair, it's much easier to stencil the whole set.

EQUIPMENT

Stencil brush

Craft knife

Sandpaper

Damp cloth

Scissors

Saucer for mixing paint

1-inch paintbrush

Felt-tip pen

¼-inch paintbrush

1½-inch paintbrush

Spray adhesive

Paint stripper (optional)

Ruler (optional)

Cutting mat

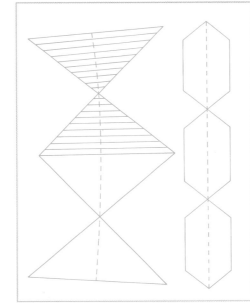

MATERIALS

❖ Old chair, already stripped, preferably with flat uprights in the backrest

❖ Acrylic paint in blue, cream, and red

❖ Clear satin varnish

❖ Sheet of stencil card or medium weight cardboard, 20 x 30 inches

❖ 2 sheets of newsprint

NOTES

This project shows you how to create a two-color stencil pattern with a symmetrical design without using any intricate measurements, as the design of the stencil is determined by the shape of the top rail and the uprights.

Newsprint is cheap, off-white pulp paper of the kind on which newspapers are printed. It is obtainable from artists' suppliers. For this project, any lightweight plain scrap paper can be used for making the stencil templates.

STARTING OUT - STEPS 1 TO 4

1 Make embossed templates for a central upright and the top rail of the backrest. To do this, lay the chair flat and place a piece of newsprint over one of the uprights. Run your fingers along its edges to give an embossed (raised) outline of the upright. Make a template for the top rail in the same way.

2 Take the embossed pieces of paper and draw around the edge of the embossed area with a felt-tip pen. You have now drawn the shape of an upright and the top rail.

3 Draw a line lengthways dividing the upright template in two, echoing the curve of the line. Do this by eye or, if you wish, you can use a ruler to help you. Along this line draw seven hexagonal shapes of the same size. Again, you can draw them free-hand or use a ruler to help you.

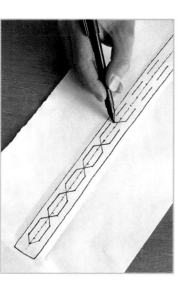

4 To make the pattern for the top rail, draw a pencil line lengthways in the middle of the top rail shape, echoing the curve of the top. Divide this line in two with a pencil line. Using this line as the center, draw a diamond shape with the felt-tip pen. Now draw about three diamonds the same size either side of the central diamond. Then, in each of the seven diamonds, draw a line from the top to bottom point.

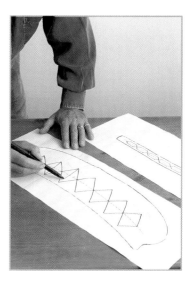

PROFESSIONAL TIP

If your chair has been painted or varnished, it may take some time to clean and prepare the surface; to save time and energy, you may prefer to have it professionally stripped. Check that any piece that has been stripped in a caustic bath has been properly neutralized afterward by treatment with a high-pressure water jet gun, which removes all traces of the acid. If this has been done, you may have to wait for the chair to dry out. The chair then needs to be sanded before stenciling.

CREATING THE EFFECT - STEPS 5 TO 8

5 You now need to make a stencil for each color of the top rail. Place a piece of newsprint on top of your design and trace the outline. Then trace half of the first diamond, skip the next two halves and trace the next two halves (a bow tie shape). Continue until you reach the end of the rail. This is pattern A. Take another sheet of paper and trace the shapes you left out in pattern A to make pattern B.

6 You now have patterns A and B and the pattern for the upright. Cut out a piece of stencil card for each of these patterns. Apply spray adhesive to the back of each pattern and stick them onto the stencil card.

7 Use scissors to cut around each of the patterns. Cut around the outside of the felt-tip outline. Work quickly so that you can prepare the stencils before the spray adhesive dries.

8 On a piece of cardboard or a cutting mat, cut out each of the stencil shapes using a craft knife. Then quickly peel the paper off the stencil card. Do this with each of the patterns.

DESIGNING YOUR OWN STENCIL

You don't have to use the stencil design that has been used here. Inspiration for your own designs may come from pattern books or traditional folk art designs from home or abroad. They may be inspired by the room in which you intend to display the chair, perhaps echoing motifs and colors of existing items of the decor, whether wallpaper, curtains, or upholstery fabric. Whatever your source of inspiration, if you want the result to be striking and stylish, follow the Golden Rule of stenciling: Keep it simple!

CREATING THE EFFECT - STEPS 9 TO 12

9 The chair needs to be thoroughly clean before you start stenciling so, if there is any old paint on it, use a good paint stripper to remove it. Sand the surface smooth with sandpaper and rub over it with a damp cloth to get rid of all the sawdust. You could have this done professionally (see tip on page 37).

10 Paint the two outside uprights with the red paint, using the 1-inch paintbrush. Allow to dry—acrylic paint doesn't take long. Turn the chair over and paint the legs and underside red as well. Clean the brush and leave the chair to dry.

11 Place the chair upright again. Paint the top rail blue, using the 1-inch paintbrush. Clean the brush, then paint the uprights that haven't been painted already with the cream-colored acrylic paint.

12 When the paint is completely dry, lay the chair down on its back. Lightly spray the back of stencil A with spray adhesive and stick it down, making sure that its edges are aligned with the rail. Put some red paint in a saucer and, using the stencil brush, paint with a circular motion to fill up each area of the stencil with the paint.

PROFESSIONAL TIP

Always use a stencil brush rather than an ordinary brush to paint a stencil. Stencil brushes are specially made with a thick round flat head and, when used vertically, either "pounced" (dabbed as if stippling and easier for beginners) or rubbed in a circular way, give full and even coverage. It is very important not to have too much paint on your brush. Always have some scrap paper at hand in order to test your stenciling brushstrokes before applying the brush to the piece you are painting.

FINISHING IT OFF – STEPS 13 TO 16

13 When this paint is dry, carefully peel stencil A off and place stencil B in position. This time, put some cream paint in a saucer and apply it using the stencil brush as in Step 12. When the paint has dried, carefully peel away the stencil.

14 Stencil the four central uprights. Lightly spray the back of the upright stencil with spray adhesive and position it on the first upright. Put some red paint into a saucer and use the stencil brush to paint into each of the stencil shapes. Peel the stencil off, position it on top of the next upright, and decorate it in the same way.

15 As a finishing touch, paint any decorative details with green paint using a ¼-inch brush. On this chair, these include the ball shapes at the top of the outer uprights, as well as the turned details on the legs. If you do not have such details, you could paint the legs and cross bars in contrasting colors.

16 When all the paint on the chair is dry, use the 1½-inch brush to paint a coat of clear satin varnish over the entire surface.

COLLECTING A SET OF CHAIRS

Old chairs vary in quality, appearance, and condition. By choosing carefully, you can make an eclectic set of chairs that are linked by a shared decoration and finish. If you want to do this, collect your set of chairs first—two, four, or six—and then work on a single chair.

When you are confident of the technique, you will find that you'll be able to paint two or three of the others within a single day. They don't need to be identical, and you can vary the stencil design or the color scheme.

COMBED SIDE TABLE

*Retrieve that old side table you relegated to the attic and turn it into a decorative
focal point with a simple but stylish combed paint decoration. Choose contrasting
colors to set off your particular color scheme.*

EQUIPMENT

Paper towel

Hairdryer

Pencil

Craft knife

Saucer for
mixing paint

Compass

Paint stripper
(optional)

1-inch
paintbrush

2-inch
paintbrush

Drafting tape,
¼-inch wide

Cutting mat

Ruler

Coarse and fine
sandpaper

MATERIALS

❖ Old square table with lower shelf

❖ Acrylic paint in turquoise, red, blue, purple,
and burnt umber

❖ Cream-colored water-base paint

❖ P.v.a. (white) glue

❖ Matte or satin acrylic varnish

❖ Drop cloth

❖ Strip of paper, at least as long as table

❖ Mounting board, 4 x 12 inches

VARIATION

❖ Acrylic paint in blue

❖ Cream-colored water-base paint

❖ P.v.a. (white) glue

❖ Matte or satin acrylic varnish

NOTE

If you are unable to purchase any drafting tape,
which is easily removed, low-tack or masking tape
makes a good substitute.

STARTING OUT – STEPS 1 TO 4

1 If necessary, use paint stripper to remove any old paint on the table top. Then, sand down the bare wood using coarse sandpaper followed by fine sandpaper for a smooth finish. Sand the legs, just lightly enough to provide a good surface for the paint. Don't forget to protect your floor from any paint spills with a drop cloth or newspaper.

2 Put some cream-colored, water-base paint in a saucer and, using the 2-inch paintbrush, paint an even basecoat on the table top and the shelf. Allow the paint to dry, then apply a second coat. Use a hair-dryer to speed up the drying.

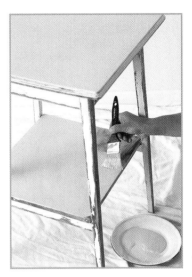

3 Mix the turquoise acrylic and cream-colored paint together in a saucer and paint each of the table legs. Paint the crossbars under the shelf and under the table top and allow them to dry. Apply a second coat of paint and allow the table to dry. Use a hairdryer to help the paint dry if you are short of time.

4 To make the design for the table top, first map out the border. Place the ruler lengthways along an edge of the table and stick down the drafting tape along the length of this side. Cut off the end of the tape with scissors, leaving a small overlap. Repeat on the other sides. For the diagonals, hold one end of the tape down in one corner and, keeping it taut, unroll it to the opposite corner. Press it down. Repeat for the other diagonal.

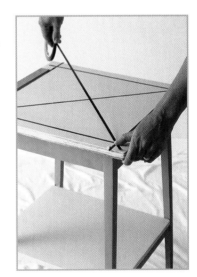

PROFESSIONAL TIP

Use a hairdryer to speed up the drying time of a coat of paint, especially since you need to apply two coats of base color before you start combing. This will enable you to complete the project in one day. Do not be in such a hurry to get started that you fail to read the label on the water-base paint can carefully. Some paints are especially quick-drying and can be ready to repaint in an hour. Always remember that two thin coats of paint not only provide better coverage, but dry faster than one thick coat.

CREATING THE EFFECT – STEPS 5 TO 8

5 Begin marking the diamond design by establishing the midpoint of one side. Place a strip of paper along one edge of the tape, so that it fits into the corner on your right. Fold the right hand end back to meet the border tape on your left, and crease the paper. Mark the table at the crease, which is the midpoint of this side. Use the same method to mark the midpoints on the other sides.

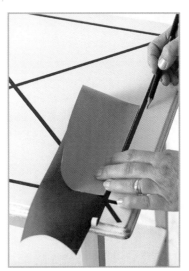

6 Join up the midpoint mark on one side with the midpoint mark on the adjacent side. Then, using the strip of paper as before, measure and mark halfway between the midpoint of each side and each corner. Use the tape to join up the marks on adjacent sides so that you end up with a pattern of diamond shapes.

7 When you have completed the design, neaten the edges by cutting off the tape that overlaps the border. Do this lightly, using a craft knife to avoid cutting into the table top. After cutting the excess tape, you can lift it by easing the craft knife under the end of the tape and then peeling it off.

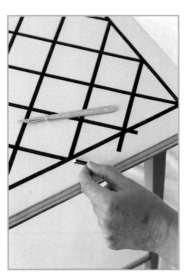

8 To make two combs, measure the width of one diamond shape on your table top. Using a piece of scrap cardboard to protect your work surface, cut out two pieces of mounting board this width using a craft knife and a metal ruler. Draw a line ¼ inch in from one edge. Make a pencil mark every ⅛ inch on this line and extend the marks to the edge of the board.

DESIGN VARIATIONS

You do not have to copy the design suggested here, but you can adapt the principles behind it to design other patterns for your table top. Using sheets of graph paper, try devising your own alternative designs. Or try adapting designs culled from other sources, such as a checkerboard square or, if you are really creative, you could make a backgammon board! Remember that when working with signwriting or drafting tape, straight lines are the rule; it cannot be forced to make curves.

CREATING THE EFFECT – STEPS 9 TO 12

9 You need to cut each of the pencil lines to make the "teeth" of your combs. However, to create the space between each tooth, cut out a slight "v" at each pencil mark, so that the point of the "v" is on the mounting board and the two ends are at the edge of the board. Try to keep the "v" shapes as uniform in size as possible.

10 In a saucer, mix some turquoise acrylic paint and some cream-colored water-base paint to create roughly the same color that you used to paint the table legs. Add p.v.a. glue and water to the paint to produce a creamy consistency.

11 Using the 1-inch paintbrush, brush a coat of paint into a row of diamond shapes. It is important to paint only one row at a time otherwise you will find that the paint has dried before you are ready to comb that area. It doesn't matter if you paint on the tape, but paint carefully to avoid dripping paint in the adjacent diamonds. (If you slip, wipe the paint off with a damp cloth.)

12 Take a comb and position it along the edge of the tape in one of the diamonds. Push it down and pull it back toward you, moving it slowly from side to side. When you reach the other side lift the comb up vertically and wipe it on a piece of paper towel. Continue to paint and comb alternate rows of diamonds with this color. When you have finished, wash the saucer and the brush with water.

PROFESSIONAL TIP

The paint used at certain stages in this project is mixed with p.v.a. (white) glue and water. When p.v.a. glue is added to the paint, it gives it a translucence, which is why it is added to the paint that is combed and not to the basecoat. Water is added to the combed paint mix in order to prevent the paint from drying out before you have had a chance to comb it. As a precaution, however, avoid trying to paint too many diamonds at the same time.

FINISHING IT OFF — STEPS 13 TO 16

13 Mix red acrylic paint and cream-colored water-base paint in a saucer to make an orange color. Add some p.v.a. glue and water as before. Paint and comb the remaining diamonds, but this time use the second comb and work in the opposite direction to the blue diamonds. When combing with this color, be very careful not to drip any paint on the blue diamonds.

14 In a saucer, mix some purple and burnt umber acrylic paint together with some p.v.a. glue, leaving the paint quite thick. Paint this color around the edge of the table and on the bottom shelf. Allow the table to dry thoroughly.

15 When the paint is completely dry, peel off the tape. Pry up one end of the tape with a craft knife, lift it up and gently peel it away. Continue to lift up and peel away the rest of the tape on the top of the table. With a bit of luck you will be able to lift all the tape off in one piece.

16 Finally, give the whole table a coat of clear varnish (satin or matte, whichever you prefer) and leave it to dry. If necessary, apply a second coat of varnish and allow that to dry thoroughly before using the table.

COLOR VARIATIONS

Traditional combing is normally used to imitate the grain of natural woods; if you wish to achieve a natural look, then make use of such colors as burnt and raw umber, burnt and raw sienna, and yellow ocher. There are, however, situations in which fantasy graining (more fun!) works very well. This graining can be in any color you like. Complementary colors always work well together, so go for red and green, yellow and purple, or blue and orange. Or match colors to those already existing in your decor.

VARIATION ~ COMBING A BORDER

1 Prepare the table following Step 1 on page 43. With the 2-inch paintbrush, paint a blue basecoat on the table top and shelf. When dry, paint on a second coat and allow that to dry. Cut two combs, 2¾ inches and the other 3¾ inches wide, following Steps 8 and 9 on pages 44-45. Set your compass radius at 3¾ inches and lightly pencil an arc at each corner.

2 To complete the penciled outline around the table, use a pencil and ruler to measure and lightly draw a border around the table top. The width of the border should be the same as the width of the smaller comb, 2¾ inches wide.

3 Mix some p.v.a. glue, cream-colored water-base paint, and a little water in a saucer to the consistency of light cream. Paint one of the borders, taking care not to go over the pencil line. Before the paint has a chance to dry, position the small comb at one end of the border, press down and drag the comb toward you. When you reach the end, lift the comb straight up and wipe it on a piece of paper towel.

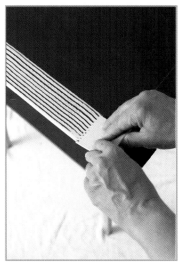

4 To complete a corner, paint within the arc, taking care not to go outside the pencil line. Position the larger comb along the left-hand side of the corner. Using the corner point as a pivot, move the comb around the arc to finish at the adjacent side. Lift the comb straight up and wipe it clean on a paper towel. Continue to paint and comb the rest of the borders and corners of the table. Allow the paint to dry. Finish with varnish.

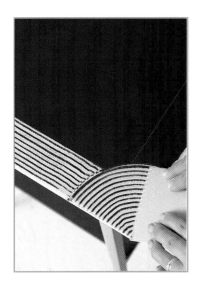

COMBING TECHNIQUES

If you have time to do so, experiment with your home-made combs. The size and spacing of the teeth can easily be varied to give a range of textures and interesting finishes. The more experimental approaches also work well in fantasy graining (see page 46). The line direction and the type of line (wiggly or straight) also give distinctively different effects. However, it is best, especially if time is at a premium, to find two or three combing techniques that you are happy and confident with and stick to them.

SCALLOPED LAMPSHADES

Strip an old, tired lampshade down to the frame and give it a crisp new scalloped parchment shade. If you don't have an old one, you can buy a metal frame from a craft shop. For a "cozier" look, cover the parchment with a colorful fabric.

EQUIPMENT

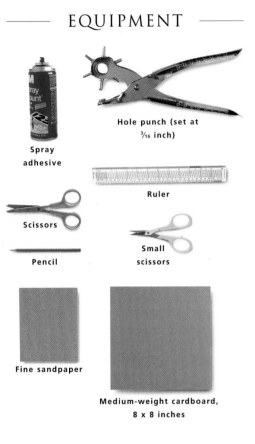

Spray adhesive

Hole punch (set at ³⁄₁₆ inch)

Ruler

Scissors

Small scissors

Pencil

Fine sandpaper

Medium-weight cardboard, 8 x 8 inches

MATERIALS

❖ Old lampshade, about 8 inches in diameter, or a new frame of the same size.

❖ Sheet of parchment paper 20 x 28 inches

❖ Double-sided tape, ½-inch wide

VARIATION

❖ Old lampshade, about 8 inches in diameter

❖ Sheet of parchment paper, 20 x 28 inches

❖ Double-sided tape, ½ inch wide

❖ Piece of fabric, 24 x 32 inches

❖ Ribbon, 24 inches long, ⅜ inch wide

NOTE

To make a different-sized lampshade, make a template out of paper first, to check if it will fit. To make a template, measure the diameter and the circumference of the largest ring of the frame of the lampshade. On a piece of paper, draw a rectangle with the height the same as the diameter of the large ring and the width one-quarter of the circumference. Measure down 2 inches from the top and make a mark on each side. Take the large ring of the frame and place it on each of these marks and draw an arc joining them. On the bottom line, make a mark 2 inches from each side, then draw a line from each mark to each end of the arc. This produces the sloping sides of the template. If your paper template is the right size for your shade, make one from cardboard and follow the project from Step 3.

STARTING OUT – STEPS 1 TO 4

1 Using a pair of scissors, cut away the covering from the metal frame of the old lampshade. You should now have two metal rings of different sizes. Remove any residue from both sections of the frame by rubbing them with fine sandpaper.

2 To make the template, enlarge the shape marked A on page 54 on a photocopier. (See professional tip on page 54.) Cut out the shape and trace around it on a piece of cardboard. Mark the positions of the holes ¼ inch in on either side; 1 inch from the top and 1½ inches from the bottom. Then, cut out the cardboard shape and punch out the holes with the hole punch.

3 Place the cardboard template on the sheet of parchment paper. Draw around it and in the holes with a pencil. Space the templates so you are able to get ten shapes from the sheet. Then, carefully cut all ten shapes out of the parchment paper.

4 Place each parchment paper shape with the drawn holes face down on your work surface. Stick a length of double-sided tape along one edge of each of the parchment paper shapes. Make sure that the edge of the tape is flush with the the edge of the parchment paper. Cut off any excess tape with scissors.

PROFESSIONAL TIP

Parchment paper does not have a noticeable "grain," so you do not need to worry about it. However, if you choose to make a lampshade from a medium-weight paper or from a very thin card, when you position the template on the paper, make sure it is aligned with the grain of the paper. This will ensure that each of the segments bends easily and will not crinkle when the lampshade is made. If you bend the paper in opposite directions, the grain will run along the bend that offers the least resistance.

PUTTING IT TOGETHER - STEPS 5 TO 8

5 To assemble the shade, first select two parchment paper shapes, with the drawn holes face up. Peel the backing strip from the double-sided tape on one shape. Then carefully line the two pieces up so that the exposed adhesive strip of the first shape sticks to the bare edge of the second.

6 Continue joining the rest of the shapes together in a similar fashion. Always remember to make sure that the drawn holes on the parchment paper shapes are face up when they are joined.

7 Finally, when all the parchment paper shapes have been taped to each other, complete the circle by joining the tape on the last piece of parchment to the bare edge of the first shape.

8 Punch out the holes in the parchment paper shapes. These will eventually accommodate the metal rings of the frame. Hold the shade at one of the joins, or "ribs", and position the hole punch carefully so that the drawn holes are aligned. Then punch through the two layers of parchment paper. Repeat until all the holes have been punched out.

PAPER FOR LAMPSHADES

Parchment paper is a thick, sturdy material with a smooth texture that is similar to plastic. It is usually available from craft shops and art supply stores. If you are unable to buy any, or if you opt for a different kind of paper, make sure the paper you buy has sufficient strength and flexibility. Some craft shops sell proprietary lampshade laminates that are stiff and translucent, and you can use these as a basis for an applied fabric or paper cover. Try using one of these in conjunction with a decorative handmade grass paper.

PUTTING IT TOGETHER – STEPS 9 TO 12

9 In order to locate the metal rings in the holes you have made, you need to make a small incision into each hole. Using small sharp scissors, make cuts into the holes at an angle of 45° to the ribs. The parchment paper will be strong enough to hold the shade on the metal frame when it is slotted into position.

10 Now turn the shade inside out by holding the ends of a rib on either side of the shade and pulling outward and down. The top will come toward you and the ribs and the holes will now be on the inside of the shade.

11 Turn the shade upside down on the work surface. Take the smaller metal ring and gently push it into the top row of holes, taking care not to damage the paper. In the same way insert the larger metal ring into the lower row of holes.

12 Finally, turn the lampshade the right way up again and space out the parchment shapes evenly around the frame. You can then place the new shade on your lamp base.

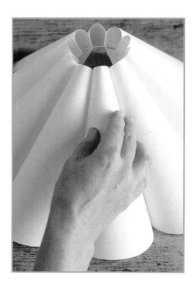

SAFETY

It is important to remember not to use powerful light bulbs with your parchment shade. Choose one that is 40 watts or less. If you use a higher wattage, the lampshade will become discolored or, even worse, may have a hole burned through it. Make sure that bases are solid and not in a position where they may easily be knocked over. If you have chosen an old lamp base that you bought in a junk shop, as a precautionary safety measure it is worth having it rewired. Have this done by a qualified electrician.

TEMPLATE A

TEMPLATE B

PROFESSIONAL TIP

This template fits a lampshade made from two metal rings 8 inches and 3 inches in diameter. It can be enlarged as necessary to fit your frame, simply by using the enlarging facility on a photocopying machine. Calculating the necessary percentage of enlargement is simple. If, for example, you wish to make a lampshade 10 inches in diameter, you will need to enlarge the template by 20 percent. Alternatively, make your own templates following the instructions on page 50.

VARIATION — A TARTAN SHADE

1 Prepare the metal frame from an old lampshade and make a cardboard template as before, but this time use template B. You should also iron your fabric now if it has any creases and leave it to cool on a flat surface. Then, working in a well-ventilated area, cover one side of the parchment paper with spray adhesive.

2 Lay the fabric down flat on your work surface. If the fabric has a "right" side and a "wrong" side, it should be laid out "right" side down. Set the parchment paper onto it, adhesive side down. (If your fabric has a pattern with lines on it, make sure that these are aligned with the edges of the paper.) Then, smooth out any air bubbles with your hands.

3 Use the template to draw 10 shapes on the paper-backed fabric and do not forget to draw in the holes. Cut out each of the shapes and punch out all of the holes, including the additional holes at the top. To assemble the shade, stick the shapes together with double-sided tape, following Steps 5 to 8 on page 52.

4 Make cuts at the holes for the metal rings using the small scissors (see Step 9, page 53). Then, lay the shade flat and thread the ribbon through the middle set of holes, leaving the ends of the ribbon dangling on the fabric side of the shade. Turn the shade the right way out and insert both frame pieces. You can then pull the ribbon and tie it into an attractive bow.

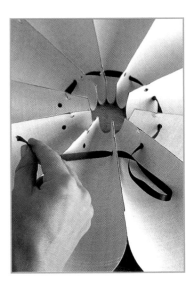

CHOOSING A FABRIC

You can cover your lampshade with a fabric of any texture, thickness, or color. To add texture to your lampshade, try using raw silk or taffeta. For a modern look, try a translucent metallic material. Or, if you are on a budget, use scraps of alternate fabrics. Really crafty lampshade makers could cut the ribbon trimmings into appropriate lengths and glue them to the top and bottom of each segment between Steps 3 and 4, thus avoiding threading. Do not use a bulb stronger than 40 watts with a fabric shade.

GILDED PICTURE FRAMES

Revamp old picture frames with simple gilding techniques. Using imitation gold and silver leaf, you can create either a convincing "Old Master" look with a gilt frame or opt for an up-to-the-minute decorative silver inlay.

EQUIPMENT

Small dish or saucer for mixing paint

Talcum powder

Rubbing alcohol

Piece of silk cloth

Damp cloth

Stencil brush

Scissors

1-inch paintbrush

Plastic wrap

Sable paintbrush No. 8

Toothbrush

Ruler or straight length of wood

Fine-gauge steel wool

Cutting mat

Fine sandpaper

MATERIALS

❖ Wooden picture frame with molding

❖ Acrylic paint in red oxide and burnt sienna

❖ Synthetic acrylic gold size

❖ Dutch metal leaf (book of 25 sheets), 6 x 6 inches

❖ Rottenstone

❖ Shellac

VARIATION

❖ Aluminum leaf (book of 25 sheets), 6 x 6 inches

❖ Synthetic acrylic gold size

❖ Acrylic paint in blue

❖ Shellac

NOTE

Gilding with Dutch metal is inexpensive and needs no special tools. This makes it a perfect medium for practicing the technique of using metal leaf. When you have perfected using imitation leaf, you may want to try your hand at real gold leaf. Try out a course first before investing in the special tools required for gold leaf.

STARTING OUT – STEPS 1 TO 4

1 To prepare an old frame, sand the surface, pushing the sandpaper into the molding in order to clean out any grease or grime accumulated over the years. Once you have sanded it as smooth as possible, wipe the frame down with a damp cloth to remove the dust.

2 Paint on a coat of shellac using the 1-inch paintbrush. This dries quickly, so brush on an even coat in one direction, avoiding overlapping areas of the frame. Clean your brush immediately after use with rubbing alcohol.

3 For the basecoat, mix together one part red oxide paint and two parts burnt sienna paint in a saucer. Add a little water to create a smooth consistency. This basecoat not only hides the surface of the wood but will enhance the patina of the leaf when it is polished. You will need enough paint to cover the frame at least twice.

4 Paint the basecoat onto the top and sides of the frame with the paintbrush. Once the paint has dried, give it a light rub with fine sandpaper, wipe off the dust with a damp cloth and apply another coat of basecoat. You should paint at least two coats, but you can apply as many as you need to get a really smooth surface. Remember; let the paint dry and sand the frame in between coats.

PREPARING THE SURFACE

When gilding an object, the more time you spend preparing the surface you are working on, the better the end result will be. It is important to make sure that the surface is absolutely free of dust and grease and that any holes, dents, or scratches are filled in and sanded, level with the surface. You need to create as smooth a surface as possible. Gilding does not mask imperfections in the way that a coat of paint does because the frail leaf picks up every detail on the surface.

CREATING THE EFFECT - STEPS 5 TO 8

5 When the final coat of basecoat has dried, paint on a coat of shellac and allow it to dry. This will stop the acrylic gold size from soaking into the frame. Clean the paintbrush immediately in rubbing alcohol. When the coat of shellac is dry, rub the frame very gently with steel wool to produce a really smooth surface.

6 Paint on the acrylic gold size evenly. Take care not to create puddles in the crevices of the molding. Paint the sides and the underside of the frame as well as the front. The size will stay in a tacky state, giving you enough time to apply the leaf before it dries.

7 The Dutch metal leaf needs to be cut into manageable pieces. Place a piece of cardboard underneath the book of leaves on the work surface and, using scissors, cut a strip about 2 inches wider than the frame, to take account of the crevices of the molding. Lay the pieces of leaf on the cardboard in a small neat pile; do not cut more than you need, but cut a few strips at a time.

8 Dust your hands lightly with talcum powder. Carefully lift a piece of leaf off the pile by picking up a corner with each hand. As you slowly lift it do not cough or blow on the fragile leaf because it crumples easily. Hold it taut to avoid creating crinkles, but not so tightly that you cause it to tear.

PROFESSIONAL TIP

Real gold and silver leaf, apart from being expensive, are extremely difficult to handle and require experience and special tools. However, Dutch metal and aluminum leaf are inexpensive, stronger and easier to use, and do not need special tools for application. Avoid touching Dutch metal or aluminum leaf with your fingers too much; use a brush if you need to move it. To avoid leaving fingerprints on the leaf, lightly brush your hands with talcum powder before handling it.

CREATING THE EFFECT – STEPS 9 TO 12

9 Hold the leaf vertically over the frame so that the bottom of the sheet is on the work surface and against the inside of the frame. You will find that the size will "pull" the leaf toward it. Lay the leaf slowly down onto the first horizontal surface of the frame. Use the soft sable brush to gently coax it down, making sure it is completely flat against the surface. Don't worry if the leaf breaks. It can be patched up later.

10 Make sure you tuck the leaf underneath the frame and brush it into the crevices of the molding. Continue laying sheets of leaf in this way on each side of the frame, cutting more strips of metal leaf as required. To gild the corners, lay a piece of leaf across the corner and gently tear it to fit. Avoid getting size on the brush as you brush down the leaf.

11 After the whole frame is covered in leaf, press the leaf down firmly so that it sticks to the size. Lay a piece of plastic wrap over the surface and use a stencil brush to brush the leaf down, in one direction only. Use a toothbrush over the plastic wrap to push the leaf into the crevices of the molding. Continue around the whole frame, making sure that all the leaf is stuck down.

12 Slowly remove the plastic wrap and carefully brush away the excess pieces of leaf. As you do so you will see gaps that need filling in. Use the excess pieces of leaf to fill these gaps, brushing them into place. Go over these areas with the plastic wrap and stencil brush or toothbrush to stick the leaf firmly down. Avoid touching the gilding with your fingers anywhere on the frame while doing this.

PAINTED FINISHES ON GOLD LEAF

Gilded surfaces can be colored as well as antiqued. To color the surface, you first need to seal it with either a coat of varnish or shellac and leave it to dry thoroughly. Then mix three parts of your chosen colored pigment with one part varnish and, using a soft brush, gently stipple the mix onto the frame. Once this coat has dried, rub over it very gently with a fine-gauge steel wool in order to reveal bright metal patches. For methods of antiquing using rottenstone or colored pigments, see page 62.

FINISHING IT OFF – STEPS 13 TO 16

13 Using a piece of tissue paper from the book of metal leaf to hold the frame steady, wipe the gilded surface gently with a piece of silk. This will make sure that the leaf is stuck down and will brush away any excess leaf. Be careful not to wipe too hard or you will snag the surface.

14 The frame can now be sealed. Brush on an even coat of shellac in one direction on the front and the sides of the frame. Leave the frame to dry. Once the frame is dry it can be safely handled. Remember to clean your brush with rubbing alcohol after use.

15 To add a patina of age and to tone down the gilding, lightly brush on some rottenstone. Brush a thick layer into the crevices of the moulding, then turn the frame over and shake off the excess.

16 Finally, polish the frame with the piece of silk cloth, polishing the highpoints well and leaving the darkness of the rottenstone in the crevices.

ANTIQUING ON GOLD OR SILVER LEAF

Rottenstone, which is available from craft shops, is ground-up weathered limestone used for polishing metal and for producing an aged effect. It can either be dusted on with a brush or mixed with varnish to make an antiquing medium. Other dry pigments, especially earth colors such as burnt and raw umber or burnt and raw sienna, will antique gold and silver leaf in the same way as rottenstone. Before antiquing, always seal a gilded surface first with varnish or shellac.

VARIATION - A MODERN LOOK

1 After sanding down the frame and dusting it off with a damp cloth, paint a coat of shellac on the front and sides of the frame and allow it to dry. Then, brush on an even coat of blue paint and allow it to dry. Lightly sand it and paint on a second coat. When the second coat of paint is dry, brush on a top coat of shellac.

2 To paint a zigzag pattern: Brush on a line ¼ inch in from the inner and outer edges of the frame, using a length of wood or ruler as a guide. Next, paint a diagonal line across each corner. Measure the distance between corners and evenly space out a zigzag line around the frame. Paint a dot of size in the corners of each triangle formed by the zigzag.

3 While you wait for the size to become tacky, cut the aluminum leaf into strips and place them on a piece of scrap cardboard or tissue paper in a pile. When the size is ready, place the strips on the frame as in Step 9 on page 61. Cover the frame with a layer of plastic wrap and press the leaf down into position using a stencil brush as in Steps 11 and 12 on page 61.

4 When the frame is covered in aluminum leaf, brush off the excess with a silk cloth, leaving the aluminum leaf stuck to the frame in the zigzag pattern. Finally, seal the frame with a coat of shellac. Once this has dried, the frame can be handled.

TRYING DIFFERENT PATTERNS

You can experiment with different patterns before gilding your frame. Try swirls, dots, or spiral shapes. Or try a combination of both aluminum and gold leaf. Once you are happy with your pattern, copy it onto your frame. Be particularly careful about how you apply the size. If you make a mistake with it, you cannot wipe it off. You can also use different colors. Strong colors, such as red or yellow ocher, usually work best with gold leaf, while green, orange, or black go well with aluminum leaf.

STENCILED TOY CHEST

A colorful stenciled clown is the star turn that enlivens an old wooden chest, giving it a new role in the nursery or playroom. Follow our color suggestions or get your kids to choose their own. Next on the bill come a jumble of jolly jungle animals.

EQUIPMENT

Spray adhesive

Cutting mat

Stencil brush

2-inch wide paintbrush

Tape measure

Craft knife

Pencil

Damp cloth

Paint stripper (optional)

Sandpaper

MATERIALS

❖ Old wooden chest, the one used here measures 11¼ x 16¾ x 27¾ inches

❖ Two pieces of stencil card, 20 x 30 inches

❖ Acrylic paint in lemon yellow, cadmium red, turquoise, crimson, cerulean blue, green, white, magenta, and yellow ocher

❖ Water-base paint in off-white

❖ Satin acrylic varnish

VARIATION

❖ Three pieces of stencil card, 20 x 30 inches

❖ Acrylic paint in lemon yellow, cadmium red, turquoise, crimson, cerulean blue, and emerald green

❖ Water-base paint in buttermilk and orange

NOTES

Because stencil card is soaked in linseed oil, making it waterproof, it can be used again and again. To make it last even longer, paint a coat of shellac onto both sides.

The upper part of the clown design on page 74 is enlarged and transferred onto the top of the box, while the lower part is enlarged and transferred to the front of the box.

STARTING OUT – STEPS 1 TO 4

1 Strip the box of old paint before you start, using a paint stripper if necessary. Pay particular attention to the areas to be stenciled. Sand the surfaces smooth with sandpaper and wipe off excess sawdust with a damp cloth.

2 Mix up enough paint to thinly coat the box by combining one part water to four parts white water-base paint. Brush the paint on in the direction of the grain of the wood. The thin coat of paint means that the wood is still visible.

3 Measure the box to work out the width and length of the enlarged clown design (see below). Its length will be the combined measurements of the front and top of the chest. Use the measurements of the grid and the enlarged design on page 74 to work out the size the squares need to be (see below).

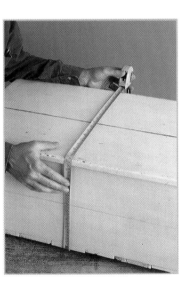

4 Draw the enlarged grid onto two sheets of stencil card, one for the top and one for the front of the box. Carefully transfer the top half of the clown design to one sheet. Transfer the drawing square by square, drawing the lines in faintly before going over them with a bold pencil line. Do the same for the bottom half of the clown.

COPYING WITH A GRID

You can copy and enlarge any picture by using this method. (If there isn't a grid over the picture, you will have to draw one over it.) First, count the squares of your grid – the clown stencil is 31 squares wide and 32 squares long. Depending on the size of your toy chest, work out how large to make each square. If each square was 1 inch, you would need 31 by 32 inches of space. Copy the grid at the required size onto a sheet of paper. Then, working one square at a time, copy each line as it appears in each square of the grid onto your own grid.

CREATING THE EFFECT – STEPS 5 TO 8

5 Place the stencil card onto a cutting mat. Using the craft knife, carefully cut out the stencil, following the bold lines. To avoid jagged edges, try to make the cuts in one flowing movement. If you are inexperienced, you can practice this technique on an offcut of stencil before you start work on the real thing.

6 From scraps of stencil card, make stencils for the corner design, border line, and juggling balls. For the corners, draw a 1¼-inch square with a rectangle ½ by 2 inches on adjacent sides. Then draw a rectangle ½ by 15¾ inches for the border line. With the compass, draw four separate circles 2¾ inches in diameter for the juggling balls. Cut out the stencils with a craft knife.

7 In a well-ventilated area, spray the back of the stencil with spray adhesive. Use the sides of the grid to position the design in the center of the top of the chest. Once you have it in the correct position, press the stencil down, making sure there are no creases.

8 You are now ready to start stenciling. Use the yellow paint straight from the tube. Load the stencil brush with a little paint and, with a circular motion, apply it in the appropriate areas of the stencil.

COLORING YOUR CLOWN

Clowns are noted for being colorful, vibrant, and jolly, and the colors you use can reflect these qualities. Red, blue, yellow, orange, green, and purple are on display in this project. However, your children may wish to choose their own color scheme and will almost certainly opt for bold primary colors. We have gone for a distressed look, toning down the original colors for the project. If you want bright colors, you can get really vibrant reds and oranges by stenciling a basecoat of yellow first, then stenciling on top.

CREATING THE EFFECT - STEPS 9 TO 12

9 Apply the red paint in a circular motion along the edge of the stencil shape. As the brush runs dry, go over the rest of the yellow. This produces the gradations in tone that lead to a three-dimensional effect.

10 Apply crimson to the tie, mouth, and eyebrows, leaving a highlight of the basecoat. Use crimson to darken the hands and eyebrows, and as a faint basecoat on the trousers and on the parts of the umbrella that will be green. For the hat, eyes, ball, and cuffs use cerulean blue. Add turquoise to the cuffs and eyes and green to the umbrella and trousers. Peel off the stencil before the adhesive sets.

11 Apply spray adhesive to the back of the clown's legs stencil and position it on the front of the box. Give the trousers a faint basecoat of crimson and, when it dries, paint them green with some turquoise shading. Mix blue and white to paint the bobbles on the shoes. Mix white and magenta to paint the shoes. Paint crimson on the ankles. When the paint has dried, carefully peel the stencil off the front of the box.

12 Use yellow ocher to paint the corner design onto the back, front, and sides of the box. Position the stencil on the top corner, hold it in place, and brush in the color. When you are re-using a stencil, wipe the top with a damp cloth after each use.

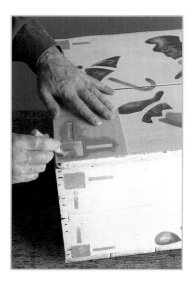

A THREE-DIMENSIONAL EFFECT

The secret of professional stenciling is a "dry" brush. Never have the paint dripping: it will seep under the stencil card and create unwelcome blobs that have nothing to do with your design. Designs do not have to be flat and two dimensional. Working with a dry brush means that the more you rub with it, the denser the color becomes. Keeping the dense areas to one side of the stencil design will create a rounded, three-dimensional effect particularly appropriate for the clown.

CREATING THE EFFECT – STEPS 13 TO 16

13 Use the long narrow rectangle to complete the border lines. Lay the stencil over the line of the corner design, hold it in position, then brush in the yellow ocher. When you are painting this line, stop short of those areas where it would otherwise go over the clown design.

14 Next, to create the effect of juggling balls, position the ball stencils at random on the sides and back of the box. Apply the paint in a circular motion to leave a highlight of the basecoat on each ball. Choose whatever colors you like for the balls.

15 When the paint has dried thoroughly, distress the box by rubbing it lightly all over with fine sandpaper. Rub just enough so that the wood begins to show through, but be careful not to rub away the detail of the clown.

16 Carefully wipe the box with a damp cloth to remove any sawdust. Then, in order to seal the design, paint the box with satin acrylic varnish. One coat should be sufficient.

DISTRESSING YOUR TOY BOX

Don't worry if your bold and brilliant colors are too much of a visual smack in the face. They can be muted and subdued by distressing your toy box. Using fine sandpaper, gently rub over the whole surface (not too hard, or you will remove all your careful brushwork), especially on the edges and corners where you should reveal some bare wood. After removing the dust with a damp cloth, varnish the box. For an antique look, use one of the tinted varnishes, such as one intended to give an old pine effect.

VARIATION - ANIMAL CRACKERS

1 Photocopy the designs from page 75. Cut around the photocopies, spray them with adhesive, and stick them onto stencil card. Cut out the stencils with a craft knife and remove the photocopies. Cut out three stencils of the background shapes (below right). Although one may suffice, the paint may flow under the stencil after repeated use and spoil it. Paint the chest following Steps 1 and 2 on page 67, using orange water-based paint.

2 Using buttermilk-colored water-base paint and the stencil brush, paint the backgrounds, which you may position arbitrarily on the box. To continue a background from the lid to the front, position half of the stencil on the lid, hold it in place and brush in the color. Keeping the stencil in position, carefully push the overhang onto the front of the box, hold it in position, and paint this area of the stencil. Leave the backgrounds to dry.

3 Now paint the six animal stencils onto the backgrounds. Position the stencil in the center of the background. Paint the polar bear turquoise, the giraffe magenta, the elephant lemon yellow with cadmium red on top, the horse purple, the monkey emerald green, and the kangaroo red. When the paint has dried, finish with a coat of varnish.

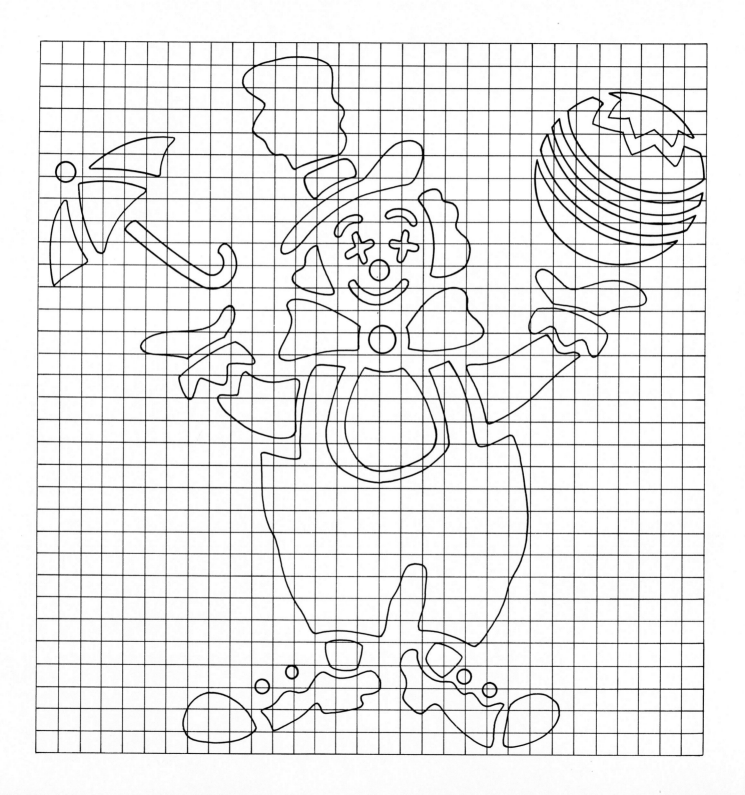

PAINTED LAMP BASES

Give junk shop finds a new identity. Transform an old-fashioned wooden lamp base with an eye-catching leopard skin design. Create a sophisticated but simple blue ceramic base with textured highlights, or brighten the nursery with a colorful polka dot lamp.

EQUIPMENT

Small piece of silk

Saucer or small dish for mixing paint

Coarse and fine sandpaper

Damp cloth

Rubbing alcohol

Sable paintbrushes Nos. 5 and 8

Fine-gauge steel wool

Scissors

1-inch paintbrush

Plastic wrap

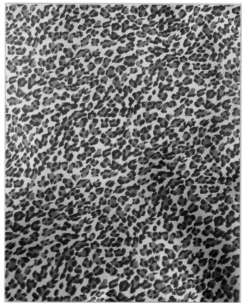

MATERIALS

For the leopard skin lamp base:

❖ An old-fashioned turned wooden lamp base

❖ Acrylic paint in white, raw sienna, burnt umber, and Venetian red

❖ Synthetic acrylic gold size

❖ Dutch metal gold leaf

❖ Shellac

For the blue ceramic lamp base:

❖ Ceramic lamp base

❖ Acrylic paint in cadmium red, cobalt blue, and white

❖ Silver sand

❖ P.v.a. (white) glue

For the polka dot lamp base:

❖ Wooden lamp base

❖ Acrylic paint in lemon yellow, hooker's green, and vermilion red

❖ Self-adhesive dot labels, ¼ inch in diameter

❖ Matte or satin acrylic varnish

NOTES

You will find it very helpful to have some reference material for the leopard skin pattern you paint onto one of the bases. You could use gift wrap, fabric, photographs, illustrations, clothing or a leopard-print bag.

Before working with the gold leaf, dust your hands with talcum powder to help stop the gold leaf sticking to your skin.

LEOPARD SKIN BASE - STEPS 1 TO 4

1 Sand the turned wooden lamp base to get rid of any old varnish and to provide a good base for the paint. Then wipe it over with a damp cloth. Mix five parts white, two parts raw sienna, and one part burnt umber with a little water in a saucer. Brush the paint onto the base using a 1-inch wide paintbrush. When this is dry, apply another coat and allow the lamp base to dry.

2 Mix three parts of raw sienna and one of burnt umber in a saucer to match the color of the dots on the reference material (page 76). Starting at the top, use the tip of the No. 5 sable brush to dab on dots of color. Work your way down the lamp base, going under and into any moldings. Keep the dots evenly spaced out, but not symmetrical. Do not paint dots on the last two rims of the molding.

3 Having cleaned the brush and saucer, mix some burnt umber and a little water. Using the No. 5 sable brush, paint a band of broken color around each of the dots. That is, follow the outline of the dot, but do not paint a solid line all the way around each one.

4 To provide a base color for the gold leaf, paint the lower two rims of the lamp with Venetian red. Use the No. 5 sable brush or, if your rim is narrow, use a smaller brush. Allow the paint to dry.

PROFESSIONAL TIP

As a precaution, put masking tape around the cord of the lamp where it enters the bottom of the lamp base. This will prevent paint from seeping onto the cord. If you are non-experienced painter, mask off the light bulb fixture, too.

When you paint the lamp, you need a steady hand. Make sure you are sitting in a comfortable position and use the table to take the weight of the arm supporting the lamp base, leaving the hand wielding the paintbrush relaxed and free.

LEOPARD SKIN BASE – STEPS 5 TO 8

5 Put some acrylic gold size in a saucer and brush it on the two painted rims. Take care not to spatter it on the dotted areas, otherwise, when you apply the gold leaf later, it will adhere to the spatters as well. You will have to wait a few minutes for the size to become tacky.

6 Keep the backing paper on the gold leaf while you cut it into smaller pieces, about 1-inch square. Pick up the squares of leaf (without backing) one at a time and place them on the sized rims, where they should readily stick. Push them gently into place with a sable paintbrush, making sure that you cover the undercuts of the molding with the leaf.

7 Next, place a piece of plastic wrap over the rims and rub them with a piece of silk to ensure that the leaf sticks to the size. Do not be too rough or you may take off the gold leaf. Finally, use a sable paintbrush to brush off the excess pieces of gold leaf.

8 To tone down the brightness of the gold and to seal the paintwork, paint the lamp base with a coat of shellac using the 1-inch paintbrush. Clean the brush with rubbing alcohol.

CHOOSING A SHADE

Careful consideration is necessary when choosing a shade. Perhaps most important is size: the lamp should not look top heavy. A slim base is set off by a petite shade, while a gutsy, robust base can support a broader, fuller shade. Shape, too, is important: a rectangular, boxlike base looks good with a pyramid-shaped shade, and rounded, bulbous bases work best with "coolie" shades. The amount of light it lets through is also an important consideration: a practical shade can suit a purely decorative lamp.

BLUE CERAMIC BASE – STEPS 1 TO 4

1 Rub the ceramic lamp base with coarse sandpaper. Your aim is to break the surface of the glaze, enabling the paint to adhere to it. It is important that you roughen every bit of the surface, so do not rush this job.

2 In a small dish, mix together equal parts of cadmium red and cobalt blue with a little water. You will need to mix enough paint for three coats. Starting at the top, paint a first coat onto the lamp base with the 1-inch paintbrush. When this coat is dry, apply another coat. Do not discard the paint that is left over.

3 While you are waiting for this second coat to dry, mix some p.v.a. glue with the remainder of the paint (one part glue to three parts paint) to make quite a thick mixture. Adding p.v.a. lightens the color of the paint, but don't be alarmed as this is only temporary.

4 Now add an equal amount of silver sand to the quantity of paint in the small dish and mix it together thoroughly. You should have a very thick mixture in your dish.

PROFESSIONAL TIP

This is a technique that works best when applied to a low-glazed or rough-textured ceramic base. A high glaze, which is prone to chipping, is not suitable. While the technique is effective and attractive on many glazed objects, it is not suitable for those that receive frequent handling. The water-base paints will last well (though not for generations!) on pieces such as lamp bases which are rarely handled, but the same is not true for plates or dishes subjected to everyday use.

BLUE CERAMIC BASE - STEPS 5 TO 8

5 Now paint on an even coat of the textured paint using the 1-inch paintbrush. Make sure you paint the top as well as the sides of the lamp base. Allow to dry. Wash the brush and saucer.

6 Squeeze some cobalt blue paint into the clean saucer. Lightly load the brush and, starting at the top of the lamp base, drag it down vertically. The high points of the textured surface pick up the blue from the brush.

7 Add some white paint to the paint in the saucer to make a paler blue color. There is no need to add water, as the paint needs to be quite thick as you paint it on the side.

8 Load the brush with paint and, as in Step 6, start working at the top of the lamp base. Lightly drag the brush down over the textured surface so that the high points pick up the pale blue from the brush. When you have gone all the way around vertically, lightly brush around the lamp base horizontally to produce a frosted effect.

TEXTURED PAINT

Simply adding a texture to a can of paint is not enough. It will sink to the bottom or flake off when the paint dries. P.v.a. glue is the binder that holds the mixture together and, being water soluble, it should only be mixed into a water-base paint. As alternatives to sand (used in this project), you can add sawdust or plaster to paint to give it texture and relief. If you make it very thick, you can give extra interest to the surface by, say, stippling it with a stiff brush or running a plastic dishwashing brush through it.

NURSERY POLKA DOT BASE – STEPS 1 TO 4

1 Prepare the surface of the wooden base by sanding it and wiping it with a damp cloth. Use the wood moldings to divide up the lamp base into bands of color. Use bright, cheerful colors straight from the tube, mixed with a little water. With a steady hand, paint the yellow areas. When these are dry, paint on the green followed by red. When the paint has dried, apply a second coat to each band of color.

2 To decorate the painted lamp base, stick on a row of self-adhesive red dots at the top of the yellow bands. Make sure the dots are equidistant, as they will act as a guide for the subsequent rows. Then stick down the next row of dots so that one dot is between the two dots above it. Continue until all the yellow bands are covered.

3 Stick down a row of yellow dots on the green band. Add other rows of yellow dots following the instructions in Step 2. Continue until all the green bands are covered.

4 To protect the paintwork and the adhesive dots, paint a coat of acrylic varnish onto the lamp base. Allow it to dry, and then apply a second coat.

DECORATING THE SHADE

The polka dot lampshade is decorated simply with a larger version of the self-adhesive dots used on the base. (These stickers come in many shapes and sizes, incidentally, so you should not feel bound to use those suggested here.) Arrange the dots in evenly spaced horizontal bands. Position the top and bottom rows first and then position the two rows in between. You can do this by eye or, if you are a stickler for precision, cut a piece of paper to the depth you want between rows and use it as a guide to positioning.

MOSAIC TABLE TOP

An unusual treatment turns an unattractive table into a visually arresting and practical bathroom feature. Choose colors to complement those of your bathroom. This might be an opportunity to use up leftover tiles from other projects.

EQUIPMENT

Jigsaw

Sandpaper

Pliers

Pencil

2-inch paintbrush

Damp cloth   **Power drill and ⁵⁄₁₆ drill bit**

Hammer

Ruler

Tape measure

Glue gun or old paintbrush and saucer   **Decorator's sponge**

MATERIALS

❖ Old table

❖ Piece of ¼-inch thick (see below) medium density fiberboard (mdf) or plywood, cut to fit your table top, the one used here measures 18⅜ x 18¼ inches

❖ P.v.a. (white) glue

❖ Panel pins, ⅝ inch long

❖ Black water-base paint

❖ Ceramic tiles, 4 x 4 inches square in white, blue, yellow, and black (see below)

❖ White tiling grout

❖ Matte or satin acrylic varnish

❖ Drop cloth or old newspaper

❖ Old cloth or dish towel

NOTE

In order to ensure that the table top is level, the tiles need to be the same thickness as the plywood. (For information about choosing tiles for this project, see the tip box on page 87.) About 12 tiles were used for this table top. You may need more or less depending on the size of your table.

STARTING OUT ~ STEPS 1 TO 4

1 Clean the table of any dirt or grime. If there is any old paint on the table, remove it with paint stripper (see tip on page 37). Sand the table and wipe off the excess sawdust with a damp cloth. If your piece of mdf or plywood is not cut to size already, measure the table top and cut the piece to fit and lay it on the table top. Refer to the tip box below if you want a molded edge to the table top.

2 Measure and mark in pencil a border 1½ inches in from the edge of the sheet of mdf. Measure along each side of the sheet, dividing each length into thirds and marking the divisions.

3 Next, using the ruler, draw pencil lines joining up the marks on opposite sides of the sheet, as shown. The area should now be divided into nine equal squares.

4 In each of the corner squares, draw another square 3½ by 3½ inches. To draw the points of the star, run the ruler from the far corner of the middle square to the opposite corner of the adjacent square. Draw a diagonal line through this square. Reposition the ruler to draw each of the diagonal lines of the points of the star.

PROFESSIONAL TIP

If your table top does not have a molded edge, you can give it a much neater finish by using a quarter-round molding, as is done in Step 8. Accurately measure the sides of your table and miter each corner, using a miter box to guide your saw. Miter boxes are not expensive and it is worth investing in one since it is not easy for the non-professional to miter a curved molding. Hold the molding in place with wood glue, and secure it with a couple of small finishing nails on each side to hold it while the glue sets.

PUTTING IT TOGETHER – STEPS 5 TO 8

5 Drill a ⁵⁄₁₆-inch hole, which is slightly wider than the jigsaw blade, into the center of the middle square.

6 Place the jigsaw blade in this hole and make straight cuts following the line of the star shape. Continue until you have cut out the entire star shape.

7 Drill a hole in the center of each of the interior corner squares and cut these out with the jigsaw. Then smooth the edges of all the cut edges with sandpaper.

8 Use the glue gun or an old brush to place dollops of glue on the underside of the mdf. Then, position the mdf on the tabletop and press it into place. Use small finishing nails to make sure that the points of the stars and the corners are fastened flat against the table top. If you wish, you can add molding around the edge of the table (see tip on page 85).

PROFESSIONAL TIP

The technique for using a jigsaw may be new to you. It is not like using a hand saw, since you cannot use a jigsaw at arm's length. You need to be looking in front of the blade to judge the direction of the cutting line. You also need to maintain a firm and even pressure to keep the shoe in contact with the wood surface and to stop the blade vibrating. Although they are not shown in this project, C-clamps are useful in steadying surfaces to be cut in situations such as this.

PUTTING IT TOGETHER – STEPS 9 TO 12

9 Using the inside "points" of the stars as a guide, pencil in a square in the middle of the table. This outlines the area of the central black square in the design.

10 Now paint the table with black water-base paint, starting with the legs and underside. When you come to the top, paint only the mdf. You do not need to paint inside the cut out shape, on the surface of the table itself.

11 Now break the tiles to make the mosaic. The safest way to do this is by wrapping them first in a cloth to prevent pieces flying about. Wrap only one color at a time, and interleave each tile with a layer of cloth.

12 Hold the tiles securely wrapped. With several short, sharp taps with a hammer, break them up into an appropriate size according to the dimensions of the design you are working to. Those used in this project are about ½-inch square in size.

CHOOSING TILES

It is important to make sure that the tiles you choose for this project are the same thickness as your table top. You will need only a few tiles so ask your local suppliers if they have any broken ones or slightly imperfect tiles that they will let you have cheaply. If you have a patterned tile that you like particularly, make sure you include some plain tiles for contrast. For a different effect, you might consider using broken pieces of a decorated china plate. For a table top you should, of course, use only the flat, central bits.

PUTTING IT TOGETHER - STEPS 13 TO 16

13 Fill in the four outside squares in yellow, white, blue, and black. Stick each piece of tile down separately. Using an old paintbrush (or a glue gun) place a dollop of glue on the back and quickly press it into position.

14 Make sure that the pieces are evenly spaced and are level with the mdf. When you have completed the four outer squares, start filling in the central square section of the star shape using black tile pieces.

15 You will occasionally find that you need to clip a bit off some pieces of tile, to make them fit. You can easily do this with pliers. Hold the tile firmly and gently and use the pliers to break off as much as necessary.

16 Fill in the two yellow points and then the two blue points of the star. Always make sure that you press the mosaic pieces firmly into place and keep checking that they are level with the surface of the mdf.

PROFESSIONAL TIP

The beauty of mosaic lies in the tightly spaced arrangement of small pieces combined to make a distinctive larger shape. Aim to fill about 80 percent of the surface with tile and no more than 20 percent with grout. Planning is essential, so before you reach for the glue, select and arrange the pieces for each part of the design to get the tightest possible arrangement. Or, cheat by sticking all the pieces face down on a sheet of paper of an appropriate size; glue their backs and remove the paper by washing it off afterward.

PUTTING IT TOGETHER – STEPS 17 TO 20

17 Using the white tile pieces, fill in the four remaining points of the star. When you have done this, run your fingers gently over the entire surface of the mosaic to make sure all the pieces are level.

18 When you are happy with the position of all the pieces, you can fix them permanently in position. Pour some grout into a dish and add a little water. Mix it thoroughly to obtain a thick paste. Be careful that you do not add too much water.

19 It is important to work quickly when applying the grout. Scoop it up on the end of the decorator's sponge.

20 Push the grout down into the spaces between the tiles with the sponge. Allow it to sink down. If necessary, add more grout in order to fill the gaps.

COLORED GROUT

Mosaic patterns are usually reliant on the effect of patterned or colored pieces of tile laid in a neutral background. It is possible to reverse this effect by using plain tiles and coloring the grouting to make it more dominant. Broken pale-colored (or white) tiles with dark grouting give a strange crackle glaze effect. You can buy grout ready colored, or you can experiment with making your own colors by adding a little powder color to a basic grout. If making your own, add color little by little.

FINISHING IT OFF – STEPS 21 TO 24

21 Before the grout has had a chance to dry, use the sponge to wipe off the excess. At the same time, continue pushing the grout down into the gaps.

22 With a damp cloth wipe off any grout that has spilled over onto the surface of the table around the edge of the mosaic.

23 Let the grout dry for about 20 minutes. Rinse the cloth clean, then use it to remove all traces of grout from the top of the mosaic.

24 Carefully repaint the mdf part of the table to cover up any stains left by the grout. When the paint has dried, give the whole table, except the tiles, a coat of acrylic varnish and allow it to dry.

CARING FOR MOSAICS

When used in a mosaic, glazed ceramic tiles and grouting can be cleaned in the same way as any other tiled surface. Remember that the surrounding table surface is made of mdf or plywood, so take care not to saturate it. Just use a damp cloth with a cleaning product if necessary. In time the grouting will inevitably discolor, but it can easily be refreshed using a proprietary tile grout whitener. You may find, however, that the slight deepening of color that comes with age is more attractive than a stark white.

WOOD-GRAIN EFFECT CHEST

A painted, bird's-eye maple effect in the central panels makes a stunning contrast to other traditional wood-graining techniques used on this simple chest. It is quick and easy to create, using glazes and a variety of brush techniques.

EQUIPMENT

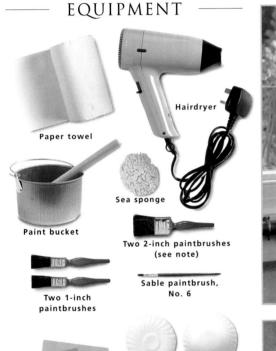

Paper towel

Hairdryer

Sea sponge

Paint bucket

Two 2-inch paintbrushes (see note)

Two 1-inch paintbrushes

Sable paintbrush, No. 6

Several small dishes or saucers for mixing paint

Coarse and fine sandpaper

1¼-inch badgerhair (or other very soft) paintbrush

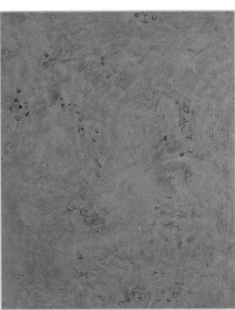

MATERIALS

- ❖ Old chest, this one measures 24 x 14 x 24 inches
- ❖ White vinyl silk water-base paint
- ❖ Acrylic paint in ultramarine, raw umber, yellow ocher, and Venetian red
- ❖ Acrylic scumble glaze
- ❖ Polyurethane eggshell varnish
- ❖ Bowl of water

NOTES

Vinyl silk emulsion paint is used as a base as it will not absorb the glaze when it is painted on top.

Keep one of the 2-inch paintbrushes dry, as you need a dry brush in Step 21.

92

STARTING OUT – STEPS 1 TO 4

1 Sand the chest and wipe it clean with a damp cloth. In the paint bucket, mix together one part ultramarine, one part raw umber, and five parts white water-base paint. Use a 2-inch paintbrush to paint this light blue basecoat onto the chest. Do not paint the basecoat on the two front panels. Wash out the paint bucket and the paintbrush.

2 To make the basecoat for the two front panels, mix up two parts of yellow ocher, one part Venetian red, and five parts white water-base paint in the paint bucket. Paint each panel with an even coat using one of the 1-inch paintbrushes. Allow the chest to dry, using a hairdryer to speed the drying, if necessary.

3 When the chest is dry, mix up the glaze for the panels in a small dish, adding one part raw umber acrylic paint to 10 parts scumble glaze. After you have mixed the two together, check the color against the close-up on page 92. If it is too dark you can add some more glaze.

4 Brush the glaze onto one of the panels. Start at the top, working your way out to the edges. The basecoat will still be visible through the glaze. Do not start on the second panel until you have completed up to Step 13 on the first.

PROFESSIONAL TIP

Any surface flaws such as dents and rough grain will show through your graining and painting, so use a quick-drying filler on any problem areas, sanding it smooth before starting on the real creative work. A little extra effort at this early stage pays off in the long run since the end result is so much more pleasing. The scumble glaze is effective only on a non-porous surface. Traditionally oil-based eggshell paints were used, but modern water-base latex or vinyl paint does the job and dries much faster.

CREATING THE EFFECT - STEPS 5 TO 8

5 After you have painted the panel, you need to work quite quickly before the glaze dries. Take the sea sponge and dip it into some clean water. Lift it out and squeeze out the excess liquid.

6 Lightly push the damp sponge into the glaze. Then twist it and lift some of the glaze from the surface. Continue to sponge the panel in this way to make swirling patterns on the surface. Avoid making too regular a pattern.

7 Next, take the 2-inch brush and spread the bristles apart in a curve. Hold it in such a way that you maintain the curve. Then dab the brush all over the surface of the glazed panel.

8 Lightly brush in all directions over the surface with the badgerhair paintbrush. This will blend the sponge marks with the brushmarks, giving them a softer edge. Because the badgerhair brush is so soft you will not disrupt the effects in the glaze. Wash the badgerhair brush in warm, soapy water after use.

ALL ABOUT SCUMBLE GLAZE

Scumble glaze is a water-based glaze that is used in painting to apply a thin layer of color. Although acrylic paint is mixed with the glaze, it remains transparent, allowing the base color to show through. Scumble glaze stays open (wet) longer than other kinds of glazes or varnish, allowing you more time to complete various graining techniques. However, it will not remain workable forever, especially on hot days or in very warm rooms, so aim to paint the glaze and create the grain effects in one continuous process.

CREATING THE EFFECT – STEPS 9 TO 12

9 Load the No. 6 sable brush with glaze and place the brush on the panel. Twist it slightly to create a broken circle. Continue painting these dark circles randomly over the surface, both in isolation and in clusters. Wash your brush in water and set the glaze aside.

10 Allow the glaze to dry, usually about 5 to 10 minutes, but always follow the manufacturer's instructions. You can use a hairdryer to speed up the drying process if necessary. In the meantime, thin some of the glaze with an equal amount of water in a saucer. (You will need only enough for one coat.) The color of the glaze should now be a lighter shade of your original glaze.

11 Load the 2-inch paintbrush with the glaze. Squeeze off any excess glaze by pressing the bristles of the brush against the edge of the plate.

12 Wipe the brush on a piece of paper towel to remove even more of the glaze. By now, the brush should feel only damp.

WOOD-GRAINING BRUSHES

An extensive range of specialty brushes is available for different wood-graining techniques, some of which look more like combs than brushes. Study some at a paint store or an art supply store before investing in them. You may find that you can adapt worn or cheaper brushes for graining purposes simply by snipping out sections of them. It is also worth experimenting with other materials such as rags, cardboard combs, sponges, and corks (to create the knots in wood) which can also give interesting wood-grain effects.

CREATING THE EFFECT – STEPS 13 TO 16

13 Hold the brush at a right angle to the surface and create wide arcs on top of the glaze, wiggling the brush as you do so. Continue making these wavy arcs over the panel. They will add paler highlights. Allow the panel to dry.

14 Use a damp sponge to clean off any brown glaze marks from the blue areas. Now repeat the entire process on the other panel, following Steps 4 to 13. When you have finished, let both panels dry thoroughly, using a hairdryer to help you, if necessary. Wash your brushes.

15 To paint the rest of the chest, mix two parts ultramarine and one part raw umber with 10 parts of the scumble glaze in a small dish. (You need to make enough for one coat of glaze.) Paint this blue glaze carefully along the central vertical. Then position the brush at the top and drag it down through the glaze in one stroke to create vertical brushmarks.

16 Lightly brush over the paint with the badgerhair paintbrush, moving the brush in all directions. This action softens the vertical brushmarks. Continue painting and softening the brushmarks with the badgerhair brush on the other vertical areas of the chest, following the directions here and in Step 15.

BADGERHAIR BRISTLES

No other brush does the job of blending and softening the almost dry glaze in the same way as a badgerhair softener. This is the essential piece of equipment for the wood-grainer, but it doesn't come cheap. Substitute tools can be used for the preliminary stages of a graining project, but the badgerhair brush is indispensable. You will need only a small one for furniture projects and, with care, it should last a lifetime. Wash it in warm soapy water after use and store it upright.

CREATING THE EFFECT - STEPS 17 TO 20

17 Decorate the cross bars with a random grained effect, starting with the top frieze. Brush on the glaze, pushing it well into all the crevices. Then, drag the brush horizontally in one stroke, being careful not to paint over the vertical area. You should have horizontal brushmarks.

18 Push the brush away from you along the frieze to produce a grained effect. Go over it with the badgerhair brush to soften the effect. Continue to create this paint effect on all the other horizontal bars of the chest.

19 Paint the glaze around the edges of the top first, then paint it evenly over the rest of the surface. Holding the brush at a right angle above the surface, use an up-and-down dabbing movement to disrupt the surface of the glaze.

20 Hold the brush at a diagonal. Push it down into the glaze and pull it toward you before lifting it off to create an ordered series of brush impressions on the lid.

FANTASY FINISHES

You can have great fun by using graining techniques with non-woody colors. Eccentric effects are probably best reserved for small items, such as small boxes, wastebaskets and trays. When using two wood-grain effects, no matter how much you are indulging in the fantastic, resist the temptation to use two or more very bold effects in one piece for they will simply drown each other out. Note that the bird's-eye maple is offset in the project above by fairly muted surroundings.

FINISHING IT OFF – STEPS 21 TO 24

21 Drag a clean, dry paintbrush over the top of the chest from one side to the other, wiggling it as you bring it toward you. Continue brushing the top in this way, until you have covered the entire surface.

22 Soften the edges of the brushmarks on the top using the badgerhair brush. This should result in a softening of the overall wood-grain effect.

23 Before you discard your glazes, take a close look at the whole chest. If there are any small areas that you missed earlier, use the small sable paintbrush to cover them up. Don't forget to wash out your brush in water immediately after use.

24 Leave the chest to dry completely. (This could take up to one hour.) Finally, seal the chest by painting it with a coat of polyurethane eggshell varnish. Use the 2-inch brush for a quick, even cover. Allow the chest to dry. If you wish, apply a second coat of varnish.

OTHER WOOD-GRAIN EFFECTS

Lifelike graining can be time-consuming and can require a vast assortment of special tools. If you want to go in for convincing effects, invest in a special book on wood-graining techniques. On the other hand, it is amazing how successful an effect can be achieved simply by pushing a paintbrush through a wet glaze or stippling with a shoebrush and blending the paint or glaze with a soft-haired brush. Try painting a few boards with different background colors and see what difference the same glaze has on them.

PRINT ROOM FIRESCREEN

This firescreen is based on the traditional method of decorating a print room, in which images framed with designs were stuck onto walls to give the illusion of a room full of paintings. The variation shows a simpler way of using this decoupage technique.

EQUIPMENT

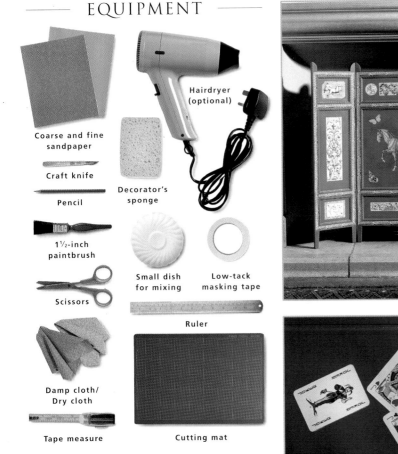

Coarse and fine sandpaper

Craft knife

Pencil

Hairdryer (optional)

Decorator's sponge

1½-inch paintbrush

Scissors

Small dish for mixing

Low-tack masking tape

Ruler

Damp cloth/ Dry cloth

Tape measure

Cutting mat

MATERIALS

❖ Firescreen, the one used here measures 24 x 31 inches

❖ Wallpaper paste

❖ Acrylic paint in opaque oxide of chromium (green) and raw umber

❖ Black and white engravings (see page 106 and Note below)

❖ Drop cloth or newspaper

❖ Large pieces of scrap paper

VARIATION

❖ Acrylic paint in raw umber

❖ Playing cards

❖ Piece of 11 x 17-inch cardboard or paper

❖ Paper glue

❖ Wallpaper paste

❖ Acrylic varnish

NOTE

A good source of images for your print room screen are published collections of copyright-free antique illustrations and designs. These are usually available from craft shops.

STARTING OUT - STEPS 1 TO 4

1 Protect your work surface from paint spills by covering it with a drop cloth or with newspaper. Prepare the surface of the screen by smoothing it down with sandpaper. Wipe it down afterward with a damp cloth to clean off the sawdust.

2 Squeeze some green paint into the bowl. Add enough water to make the paint the consistency of light cream. Make sure you mix enough paint for one coat of paint on both sides of the screen.

3 Begin by painting the moldings, brushing the paint well into the crevices in one, even stroke. Then, paint the panels until the whole screen is covered. Allow it to dry.

4 While the screen is drying, think about how you would like to arrange your cutout images. Set them out on the floor or worksurface in roughly the positions they will take on the screen. Keep adjusting them until you are satisfied with the arrangement. Make sure that the elongated border design is in keeping with the images featured on the main part of the screen.

CHOOSING THE PICTURES

Give each panel a different but unified theme, such as the garden, animals, or the sea. Consider the shape of whatever it is that you are decorating. For this project, the panels in the firescreen suggested a strong central motif, with smaller motifs for the surrounds. Border motifs need to be the right scale and repetitive. Don't choose prints that have very fine lines which will make cutting out time-consuming. Prints are usually better than photographs because they have a well-defined edge.

PUTTING IT TOGETHER – STEPS 5 TO 8

5 To work out how much border design you will need, measure the height of the frame and the length of the horizontal bars with a tape measure. Add the two measurements together for the total length of border design you will need to photocopy.

6 Work out if the designs you have selected need to be enlarged or reduced on a photocopier. To do this, mark off on a piece of paper the points where you expect the top and bottom of each image to lie. Once you have a rough idea of the size, you can reduce or enlarge the images to fit their spaces.

7 Once you have selected your designs and made them a suitable size, you can cut them out. If you are a beginner, use scissors rather than a craft knife to cut out irregular shapes; scissors are likely to give a cleaner edge if you cut in a continuous movement without lifting up the scissors from the paper.

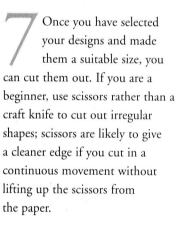

8 You should bear in mind that when selecting and cutting suitable designs there is no need to use the whole picture each time (see below). It is acceptable to choose one small detail of a larger design.

LOOKING AT DETAILS

Do not overlook large and intricate designs, as these will usually have smaller details that make interesting pictures on their own. In particular, look for medallion shapes, or pictures of the human form, such as pictures of statues in large architectural friezes. These will be easy to cut away from the main pictures. Other good sources of decoupage detail are gift wrapping (how about a festive screen) and reproductions of old catalogs with engravings. Always photocopy from the book. Don't cut up the original!

PUTTING IT TOGETHER – STEPS 9 TO 12

9 To cut out the border designs with straight edges, use the metal ruler and a craft knife (or cutting knife) on a cutting mat. Hold the ruler firmly and slide the craft knife along its edge.

10 After the images have been cut out, you need to decide on their final positions on the screen. Using low-tack masking tape, stick them temporarily in place, adjusting the position of each as necessary until you arrive at a satisfactory composition.

11 When you are satisfied with the arrangement, draw around each shape faintly with a pencil before taking them off. Use these outlines as a guide. There is no need to pencil around the borders. These will be centered on the horizontal and vertical bars of the screen.

12 Put a small amount of wallpaper paste in a small dish and add a little water until you have the consistency of heavy cream. Working on one design at a time, brush the paste into each pencil outline. Slightly overlap the edges of the outline so that you will be able to move and adjust the designs when you have placed them on the screen.

DESIGNING YOUR SCREEN

When selecting images for designs to use on your screen, you need to be able to visualize the possibilities of the image in conjunction with the screen. Once you have selected a few images you like, it may help to sketch out your design on paper first. You do not have to be an expert, just sketch the shapes of your chosen pictures. Photocopy more pictures than you need, then you can see which ones will work together. Try using the same image more than once: make one version big, the other tiny.

PUTTING IT TOGETHER – STEPS 13 TO 16

13 Place a design right-side down on a piece of scrap cardboard. Starting from the middle, brush the paste out to the edges until the whole surface is covered.

14 Gently lift the pasted picture off the cardboard, taking care not to tear it. Position it on the panel on the pasted area. Slide it inside the pencil marks. When it is in position, gently rub it over with a cloth to get rid of any air bubbles. Repeat the last three steps to stick the remaining designs onto the screen.

15 Before sticking on the borders, apply paste to each of the vertical and horizontal bars. Paste the back of a border design and position it centrally on the bar so that one end overlaps onto the vertical bar. Paste up another border design and position it on the vertical so that its end overlaps the horizontal border design.

16 To make a neat corner, use a craft knife to make a 45° cut (a miter) where the horizontal and the vertical borders meet. Alternatively, only cut through one of the borders if you do not mind having an overlap. Always use a sharp blade when doing this but take care not to cut the screen. Craft knife blades blunt very quickly when used for cutting wet paper, so replace them frequently.

BORDERS

Good sources for borders are architectural design books, printers' ornaments, and typographic borders. It is also possible, now that decoupage is a popular hobby, to buy readymade borders from craft shops. If you are making your own, choose one that is appropriate and enlarge or reduce it as necessary, and measure exactly how long it needs to be. Photocopy it enough times to fit onto one sheet of photocopying paper and then photocopy this sheet enough times to do the job with some to spare.

FINISHING IT OFF – STEPS 17 TO 20

17 After you have made the cut, carefully lift off the surplus paper. Reposition the two miters so they meet to form a right angle and press them down into place. If you cut through only one border, make sure the patterns of the borders meet up neatly.

18 To make the other horizontal borders neat, follow the steps for pasting the border and the screen. This time, however, trim the edge of the border so that it butts up against the vertical border design.

19 When you have pasted on all the designs and the borders, use a sponge to wipe off the excess paste from around all the pasted areas. Let the paste dry, using a hairdryer if necessary to speed this up.

20 Finally, mix two parts raw umber paint together with 10 parts of acrylic varnish in a small dish. Paint this tinted varnish onto the screen to give your print room screen an antiqued finish.

ANTIQUE VARNISHES

To achieve the smooth, glasslike finish of traditional decoupage requires a minimum of 30 coats of varnish—far more than can be completed in one day! Modern quick-drying acrylic varnishes help speed the process up a lot. They also come tinted to give an antique patina to your work. Alternatively, clear varnishes can be tinted with a small squeeze of raw umber artist's acrylic paint to achieve the same effect. Or antique your decoupage pieces first, by dipping them in a weak tea solution and allowing to dry before applying.

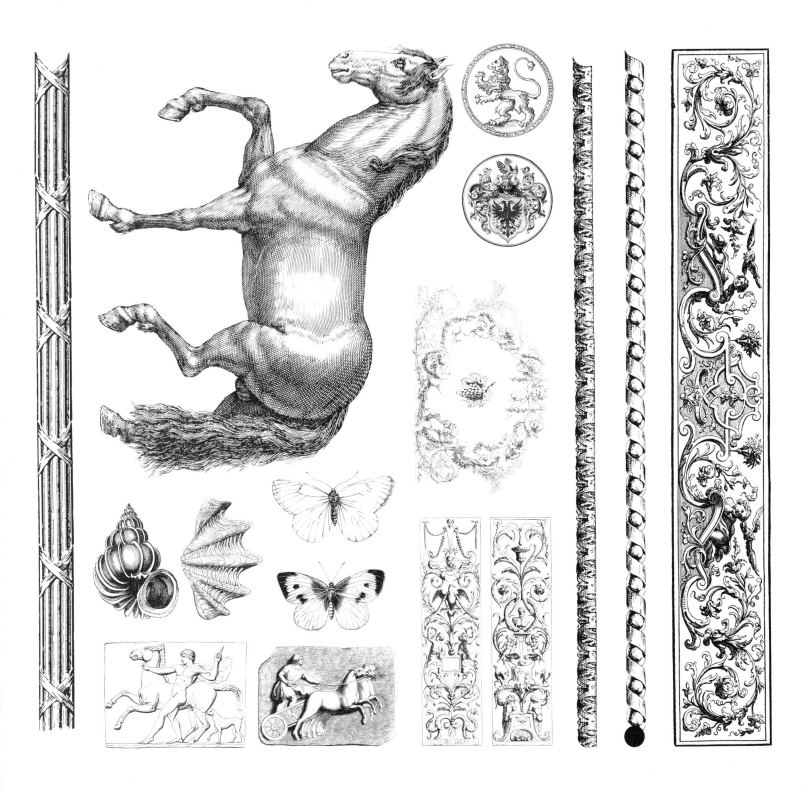

VARIATION - CARD ROOM SCREEN

1 Paint the firescreen following the steps on page 101, but using raw umber as the color, not green. While waiting for the paint to dry, arrange some playing cards on a sheet of 8½ - by 14-inch paper or cardboard. Try a royal flush or a hand of aces, as well as the jokers or other individual cards. When you think you have enough pictures for your screen, stick the cards down with paper glue.

2 You now need to make a same-size color photocopy of your design. (You can do this at a photocopying center.) Then place the photocopy on the cutting mat and carefully cut around the individual cards and the groups of cards. Straight lines are best cut out with a craft knife.

3 Arrange the pictures on the screen with low-tack masking tape. When you are happy with your arrangement, draw a pencil outline around the pictures. Apply wallpaper paste to the screen and to the back of each picture and stick them onto the screen. Use a cloth to gently smooth away the air bubbles from the paper and sponge off any excess wallpaper paste.

4 Finally, when the paste has dried, apply a coat of acrylic varnish. Leave the screen to dry, then add another coat of varnish, if necessary.

USING "FOUND OBJECTS"

Make the most of a photocopier (color or black and white) and experiment with other images and items. Old sepia-tint photographs, postcards, or even colorful foreign banknotes and coins can be used to make your screen highly personalized, perhaps as an unusual showcase for images that are particularly dear to you. Using found objects the same size can create humorous trompe l'oeil studies. Don't forget that you can enlarge images on photocopiers—old postage stamps, for example, look fantastic when enlarged.

GLOSSARY

BOLE A reddish-brown pigment, originally derived from clay. It is typically painted on a surface underneath gold leaf to enhance color when gilding.

CRACKLE GLAZE A crackled, aged effect produced by the application of two coats of glaze with different drying speeds. The end result is similar to the fine cracks on antique oil paintings.

GROUT A mortar used for filling joints between ceramic tiles to seal the surface.

JARDINIERE An ornamental pot or planter.

METAL LEAF Very thin sheets of metal produced by rolling or hammering metal. The leaf is then used for gilding woodwork and other surfaces. Real metal leaf can be quite expensive. The cheap alternative is called Dutch metal. Metal leaf is available in a number of different "metals" or colors: gold, silver, etc.

NEWSPRINT Cheap, off-white scrap paper of the kind on which newspapers are printed.

PARCHMENT PAPER A thick, sturdy, translucent material, with a smooth texture.

PATINA The sheen on a surface is its patina. It is also used to describe the fine layer of oxide formed on metal, such as verdigris.

P.V.A. (WHITE) GLUE A white, odorless glue that dries clear. It can be mixed with paint to seal the surface of objects. P.v.a. glue is also known as woodworking glue, school glue and white glue.

ROTTENSTONE Ground-up weathered limestone used for polishing metal. When used with gilded objects, it produces a dusty, aged effect.

SCUMBLE GLAZE Water-based glaze used in painting to apply a thin layer of color (when mixed with pigment). The glaze is slow to dry and can be dabbed, rolled, or sponged to provide a number of different paint effects.

SHELLAC A yellow resin secreted by the lac insect, dissolved in ethanol or a similar solvent to produce a varnish.

SIZE A special glue, usually translucent white in color and the consistency of thin cream. It is most typically used in gilding.

STENCIL CARD Card that has been soaked in linseed oil to prevent the absorption of paint, enabling the stencil to be used again and again. To further protect stencil card, you can also paint it with shellac.

TRANSFER PAPER Paper with chalk backing used to transfer patterns onto irregular objects. The chalk leaves a tracing, which can then be painted.

TROMPE L'OEIL A style of painting or decoration where a picture is a convincing illusion of reality.

WUNDASIZE A brand of size commonly used in gilding.

INDEX

FANTASTIC FIX-UPS: *Acknowledgments*

The author would like to thank and acknowledge the hard work of
the following people:

Sally Walton for being my wife; **Stephanie Donaldson** for styling and
allowing us into her home; **Jane Scrutton** for also allowing us into her
home; **Paul Roberts** for his craftsmanship and **Steve Differ** for always
being there with a helpintg hand.

Marshall Editions would also like to thank **Sophie Sandy** for editorial
assistance and **Philip Letsu** for design assistance.